W9-CES-644

relief for the body, renewal for the soul

A Doctor's True Stories of Healing and Hope

G. SCOTT MORRIS

PARACLETE PRESS
BREWSTER, MASSACHUSETTS

Library of Congress Cataloging-in-Publication Data

Morris, G. Scott, 1954–
    Relief for the body, renewal for the soul / G. Scott Morris.
        p. cm.
    ISBN 1-55725-269-6
    1. Medical care—Religious aspects—Christianity. 2. Church work
with the sick—Case studies. 3. Pastoral medicine—Case studies. I.
Title.
    RA975.R44 M67 2001
    362.1—dc21   00-012094

Published by Paraclete Press
Brewster, Massachusetts
www.paracletepress.com

Printed in the United States of America

Contents

*To Bill Morris, my father, who taught me that "everybody wants a
pat on the back. I want it, you want it, a dog wants it."*

Acknowledgments

While this book records my own experiences with a group
of God's children over the last thirteen years, there are a
number of people I wish to thank for making the book a
reality. My now retired assistant, Barbara Lindstrom, read
my longhand version and typed the manuscript, but, more
importantly, she encouraged me every day. Charla Honea
helped form the writing style I adopted. Lori Jackson
helped with editing the early drafts. Linda Roghaar, without ever meeting me, agreed to be my agent, and the folks
at Paraclete Press accepted the stories of my life and agreed
to publish them.

A special thanks to Phyllis Tickle who covinced me I had
a story worth telling, and to Mary Gilleland who has
helped with many details in the long process of publication.

Mostly I wish to thank the staff, patients, volunteers,
and friends of The Church Health Center whose lives have
mingled with mine and whose stories I tried to tell.
Together we have sought the mystery of God's unveiling
the beauties of life.

And finally, I am grateful to Katherine, my wife, for helping bring into existence what was only a dream.

A Note about
The Church Health Center

In seeking to reclaim the biblical commitment to care for the poor who are sick, Scott Morris, M.Div., M.D., opened the doors to The Church Health Center in Memphis, Tennessee, in 1987. Today, The Church Health Center cares for over 30,000 patients per year—children, the elderly, the homeless, and the working poor.

Through Dr. Morris's efforts, health care professionals, volunteers, pharmaceutical companies, hospitals, corporations, foundations, and faith congregations have joined hands to provide medical, dental, and eye care; pastoral counseling; an affordable health care program offered to employers of low-wage workers; and a new preventative medicine program called Hope & Healing. The Church Health Center has answered a call greater than Dr. Morris ever imagined and has made Memphis a healthier community in body and spirit.

Over the past several years Dr. Morris and The Church Health Center have been featured on the CBS Evening News, CNN, and PBS's "Religion and Ethics Newsweekly," and in the *Journal of the American Medical Association*.

Introduction

"It was really a fine old house in its day. If you look closely you can see all the woodworking detail. They just don't build houses like this anymore."

The real estate salesman was almost a caricature. It was all I could do to keep from laughing. We were looking at a falling-down boarding house that had not been cleaned up in years. Every room had been subdivided into two, padlocked apartments, each barely big enough to hold a bed. Two old tires and a television with a broken picture tube lay scattered in the living room.

Underneath the stairway was an oddly placed bathtub whose shower spigot never stopped dripping. Most people would have laughed if they had known what I was thinking. *This is the perfect place*, I thought to myself. *It's ideal*. I could see in this falling-down house everything I needed in a location to make my lifelong dream of creating a church-based health clinic for the working poor come alive.

As we walked up the stairs, the agent told us the house's history. It had once been the home of Wassell Randolph, a prominent Memphis lawyer and member of the library board, for whom the University of Tennessee's student center is named. As he got older, he was unable to climb the stairs and lived only on the first floor. The awkwardly placed bathtub had been installed for him during his last years.

On his death, the house was divided into increasingly smaller rooms. At one point, twenty elderly people lived in what was built as a four-bedroom house. The police eventually closed it down as a boarding house when a family member complained about the poor living conditions. Next it was a brothel. Directly across the street from St. John's United Methodist Church, once Memphis's most prominent Protestant church, this was an odd place for such a business, but times change. The church membership had shrunk as the wealthy moved out toward the East. Even the business for ladies of the night was not that good, so they, too, moved on. When we visited, a group of young actors from a local theater troupe lived in the house.

As we walked from one room to the next, I tried to envision the original architecture of the house. Hints of its former beauty were everywhere: the twelve-foot ceilings, the hand-carved moldings, and the hardwood floors. But now, rotting drywall and flaking paint marred its former glory.

Thinking that the building was empty, the real estate agent opened the door to the attic stairway. We were walking up the stairs, still talking about the history of the house, when I noticed that we were not alone. Heavy breathing and sighing came from the room at the top of the stairs. "John, you said everyone was gone," murmured a young woman.

"Excuse us," we called out, descending the stairs and agreeing that we could see the attic another day.

Later, as we stood in the yard trashed with odds and ends, the agent asked, "Well, what did you think?"

Frank McRae, the minister at St. John's, and Zeno Yates, an architect who had volunteered to help me design a clinic, both looked at me. Without hesitation, I responded, "We'll take it."

The Church Health Center had a home. For fifteen years I had been dreaming of a way to fulfill the church's biblical call and historical mandate to care for the poor—body *and* spirit. Through seminary and medical school I waited for this day to finally begin, but in many ways my dream had begun when I was eight years old. One Sunday morning the pastor of my church came up to me, patted me on the head, and introduced me to his brother.

"Yes sir, this boy is going to make a fine preacher one of these days." As corny as it sounds, from that day on I never thought of being anything other than a minister. I knew that I did not want to preach every Sunday, but what else could I do?

Over the next ten years I read the Bible and focused on the recurrent themes of healing the sick and caring for the poor. I could not, however, see how my own church followed that calling to heal. We prayed for people on Sunday morning. The pastor was expected to visit the people in the hospital. A few people visited the shut-ins. That was our healing ministry, but that was not enough. At the same time, I would watch Oral Roberts on TV every Sunday morning and was dismayed by his attempts to heal the blind and the lame. There must be another way. I was determined to find it.

After finishing college, I attended seminary at Yale Divinity School where I spent most of my time studying and thinking about the church's role in health care. Fortunately, Yale did not see my dream as offbeat and encouraged my pursuits. Rather than learn Greek and Hebrew, required courses at many seminaries, I studied chemistry and physiology and tried to understand their relationship to the human spirit and God's will. In Bible courses, I wrote papers on the healing stories that fill almost every page of the New Testament.

One day while sitting in the chaplain's office for Yale Medical School, I saw a pamphlet that was to change my life. The title was *How to Start a Church-Based Health Clinic*. That was it! That was what I wanted to do with my life. Written by Granger Westberg, the pamphlet was only twenty pages long, yet its basic idea of a church-based health clinic captured my imagination and has never left me.

The next day I was on the phone to Granger, a Lutheran pastor from Chicago, asking him a thousand questions. I was soon to learn that Granger was the inspiration for many people interested in faith and medicine. The next summer I flew to Chicago to meet him. Later, while in medical school, I spent a month at his clinic in Hinsdale, Illinois, learning all I could about his views of *whole* person health care. At last I had a concrete idea about how to begin binding body and spirit.

While I was intrigued with the concept of a health clinic based on the church caring for both the body and the spirit, I did not agree with the location of Granger's original clinic in a wealthy suburb. Sensing my uneasiness, Granger told me about a young doctor who had begun a clinic to serve the poor of Washington, D.C. Her name was Janelle Goetcheus, one of only three living saints I have ever met. As soon as possible, I was off to Washington to meet her.

When I arrived I rented a car, took out a map, and began looking for Columbia Road. I had driven in Washington before and thought I knew my way around, but I had not driven through the poor neighborhoods. When I finally found my way to the Columbia Road Health Clinic, I was fifteen minutes late for my appointment with Dr. Goetcheus.

As I parked my car on the street, an uneasy feeling came over me. I had been eager to keep my appointment, but now I realized I was in a place that felt foreign and unsafe. As soon as I went to put money in the parking meter, a homeless man approached me.

"Hey buddy, can you spare a quarter?"

I shook my head. "No," I said quickly and walked briskly away, not looking back. I thought to myself, *Why in the world am I here?*

I read the name over the door, Columbia Road Health Clinic, and walked into the waiting room. It was filled with crying children. Almost no one spoke English. I walked to the receptionist and said, "My name is Scott Morris. I'm here to see Dr. Goetcheus."

The phone rang; she answered in Spanish and began a lengthy, animated discussion, then finally returned to me.

"Who did you say you are?" At that moment, I was wondering myself who I was. I repeated my name. "Oh, Dr. Goetcheus wants you to meet her over at S.O.M.E."

"What is S.O.M.E.?" I asked.

"So Others May Eat. It's a soup kitchen where we also have a clinic. It's not very far away."

She gave me directions, and I got back in my car. I drove through forgotten and decaying neighborhoods until I arrived at my destination, a newly restored warehouse-looking building.

I opened the door and again asked for Dr. Goetcheus.

"She's with a patient, but you can wait in the lab." By now I was becoming tired and frustrated, but I waited nonetheless. The room had the smell of a strange mix of body odor and alcohol. It was clean, but the instruments looked old. Many of the shelves were empty.

After about ten minutes, a small, plainly dressed woman with a cross around her neck emerged from the room. She reached to shake my hand and in a soft voice said, "Hello, I'm Janelle. I'll be with you in a minute. I just need to finish with this patient."

I wasn't sure what to make of her. She was certainly not an imposing figure, and she did not at first seem too charismatic, an assessment I was soon to reconsider.

When Janelle returned, she gave me her full attention and answered all of my questions. She had planned to be a medical missionary, but when she learned of the Church of the Savior's desire to begin its own health clinic, she was persuaded to start her medical mission in Washington, D.C.

She began seeing patients out of a two-room apartment until she found the money, with the help of the church, to buy and renovate an old building. The community she cared for consisted mostly of Salvadoran refugees who had come to America during the civil war in El Salvador. She learned Spanish and a new way to practice medicine. Like me, she was fascinated with the ideas of Granger Westberg but soon found many of them too tied to middle-class values to be effective among the urban poor and Central American refugees. She adapted the ideas as best she could.

Since many of her patients were uninsured, it was always an ordeal to get diagnostic tests done and to arrange for patients to see a specialist. When she first had an uninsured patient who needed to be admitted to the hospital, she took him in her own car to the hospital and demanded that he be cared for. The hospital promptly refused to admit him.

"So what did you do?"

"It seems a little foolhardy in retrospect," she said. "But he was emaciated, and weighed very little, so I picked him up in my arms, walked back into the emergency room and told them I was not leaving until he was admitted." In a quiet, sheepish voice she continued, "Within a few minutes they found him a bed." It was at that point that I changed my opinion about her charisma.

I asked why she did what she did. "It is what my Lord has called me to do. People are hurting and in need of care. God has given me the skill to offer that care. I don't see that I have any other choice."

The words she spoke touched me as nothing ever had before. While I knew I was not like Janelle, I wanted to do what she did. Yet I doubted if I had her commitment. Not only did she work among the poor, but she lived with them

as well. She took very little money for her work and
seemed never to complain. I was sure I did not have the
same resolve as she, but I was also sure that I wanted to
create a model similar to what this great spirit had created
with God's help.

With the inspiration of Janelle always near my heart and
my mind, I entered medical school with the intention of
starting a church-based health clinic for the poor. While in
medical school, I felt like a stranger in a strange land. I was
still consumed with the great questions of the nature of
God and the problem of evil. But none of my erudite
theologizing helped me on multiple-choice anatomy tests. I
was appalled to learn that medical school, during the first
two years, was all about memorizing and regurgitating facts.
Thinking seemed to have little to do with becoming a doctor,
at least not thinking in the form I had come to value.

For two years I felt alone and unappreciated. I walked
around with a bit of a chip on my shoulder. After all, I was
above the mundane and antiquated way of learning medicine,
wasn't I? Where could I discuss the things that really
mattered?

My attitude changed during my senior year when I
spent the summer in Zimbabwe. Ostensibly I was on a
research project funded by Coca-Cola to investigate ways
of predicting which pregnant women should be transported
early on from their village homes to the community hospital.
But I really went to learn how mission hospitals and local
churches in the Third World had bound body and spirit
together.

The first experience to transform my way of thinking
occurred while I worked at a Salvation Army mission station.

My mentor at the hospital was a Canadian doctor who had spent twenty years working in the bush. He was the only physician for a hundred miles.

I asked him, "How are you able to care for so many people?"

"I can only do it with the aid of the village health care workers."

These women, referred to as "barefoot doctors" in China, received six weeks of formal health care training at the mission and then returned to their villages, where they encouraged good hygiene practices and prescribed simple treatments for non-life-threatening illnesses. Once a week, the doctor visited the village in his Land Rover and treated the patients the village health care worker thought needed his attention. On the days I went with him, the village clinic was always packed. We treated as many people as we could until we were exhausted. After dark, we continued by candlelight. When someone was sick enough to be admitted to the hospital, he or she was given a seat in the back of the Land Rover to be driven back to the mission. On one visit when I went to get into the car, a man was sitting on the roof of the Land Rover.

"Why is he up there?" I asked.

The doctor smiled at me and said, "I suspect he has tuberculosis. Since you have not been inoculated against TB, would you rather ride up there? You can take your choice."

I quickly appreciated his concern for me. I also appreciated the value of the lay health worker and began to believe that there must be a way to translate the same concept to American inner cities. At the Church Health Center, we have come to call such people "lay advisors." These are women primarily from small African-American churches who were already giving out health care advice before we met them. The advice they gave was sometimes good and sometimes not so good.

We offer an eight-week training course where we teach them about high blood pressure, diabetes, the importance of prenatal care, and more. They then return to their congregation to look for medical problems that are going untreated. They are not exactly village health care workers, but they are close. This was the first of the three ways that the Third World opened my eyes to a better way of caring for people.

The second was when I met the inventor of the V.I.P.—the ventilated individual privy—a unique type of toilet that reduced the incidence of disease all over Africa. Developed by a mission doctor, the contraption was both a toilet and a shower. In the morning, the woman of the family went to the river and brought back water and placed it on the roof of the V.I.P. During the day the water was heated by the sun. When the man came home, he took a hot shower in the heated water, and the runoff from the shower filtered through the toilet.

The V.I.P. accomplished three critical tasks. It discouraged people from taking a bath in the river, usually infected with a parasite that causes a disease known as schistosomiasis or bilharzia. Heating the water killed the parasite and prevented this potentially fatal disease. Second, the V.I.P. trapped flies and other insects inside, preventing the spread of diseases carried by human feces. Finally, the V.I.P. prevented the river from being polluted by human feces.

In my mind, the V.I.P. is a wonderful example of how the best health care is more than simply giving out pills that may not even work. It shows how faithful work can extend beyond traditional church boundaries. At the Church Health Center we have been striving to emulate this model of the mission doctor, although we have not created anything so ingenious as the V.I.P.—at least not yet.

The third memorable experience was my visit with a nyanga—or witch doctor. From the time I arrived in Zimbabwe, I had asked to meet a traditional healer, but I was repeatedly put off. Finally during my last week there, I received permission from the local nyanga association to talk with a nyanga who lived, worked, and practiced his trade on a sugar cane plantation near the South African border.

I was very excited as my contact drove me to the nyanga's house. We arrived just as the nyanga, dressed in overalls after working all day in the fields, rode up on a bicycle. Standing only 5 feet 7 inches tall, the nyanga had callused hands and was muscular from cutting sugar cane for most of his 45 years.

He very politely showed us into his home, a three-room concrete brick building. He motioned us toward the back room and asked us to remove our shoes, which we promptly did. As I entered the candlelit room, I felt as though I was entering another world. I immediately noticed the smell of incense. A zebra skin and multiple snake skins hung on the wall, and a lionskin rug lay on the floor. I sat on the floor with my back to the wall. The nyanga sat directly across from me.

Once I got there, I wasn't quite sure what to ask. My interpreter helped break the ice, and then I asked about the types of ailments he saw. He seemed to treat the same sorts of illnesses as a family practitioner.

I asked him, "How do you decide what kind of treatment you use?"

"If the problem is simple and straightforward, like gonorrhea, I just take something off my shelf." He pointed to several shelves lined with jars filled with herbs and roots. "If, however, the problem is more complicated, I must consult my ancestral spirit."

I had already learned what this consultation entailed. A person became a nyanga when he or she was "possessed" by the spirit of someone who was a nyanga but who had long since died. Once a person claimed such a possession, he or she went to the nyanga association, which had the authority to verify one's claim of possession. If the association believed your claim, then you were given three patients to treat. Success was not necessarily judged on rendering a cure, but on the wisdom of your actions.

To treat a person with a complicated condition, the person sat before the nyanga and asked the ancestral spirit for help. At this point, the nyanga went into a trance and the spirit took possession of his body and spoke through the nyanga. The person was then told what must be done to be healed.

I was fascinated by this whole idea, and asked, "Could I talk with your spirit?"

The nyanga frowned. "I would very much like for you to talk with him, but my spirit lived during the rebellion of the 1890s. If he were to possess me and then see your white face sitting before me, I would have to kill you. I do not think either you or I would want that."

I agreed and continued, "Why do you think people come to see you and then immediately go to see the Western doctor?" During my stay in Zimbabwe I had noticed that this was usually the case. Even though I could not speak the language, I could often understand patients' problems because they would have fresh markings made by the nyanga on their bodies, either with a knife or ink. If the patient was having headaches, there would be cuts on his or her forehead, while a stomach ache would be indicated by a fresh design on the abdomen.

It was clear to me that people believed Western medicine was more effective than the nyanga's treatment, but they still went to the nyanga first.

The nyanga thought for a moment, then said, "They come to me because I can tell them *why* they are sick."

He was exactly right. No matter how scientific Western medicine is, it cannot answer this fundamental question of why one becomes sick. At best, science can give the cause—a virus or bacteria or an autoimmune disease, but people both in Zimbabwe and the United States long to know the answer to a more fundamental question—why?

This question is, in principle, a question of the spirit and requires a spiritual answer. For the nyanga, the patient was faulted for not properly honoring his or her ancestors and the cure involved righting this wrong. For us, an answer is not so straightforward. Some people resort to the answer, "It's God's will." While this pat answer does not satisfy me, I *do* believe that to answer the question, "Why?" we must look to spiritual and not scientific sources.

Over the years at the Church Health Center, we have
tried to bind body and spirit because we want to help
patients answer the "Why?" whenever they are sick. In
most cases, my answer to this question is never as satisfy-
ing as the nyanga's or simply saying, "It's God's will." I am
always struggling to help people through the spiritual
maze that sickness inevitably engenders.

After graduating from medical school, I was eager to
begin the church-based health clinic I had been dreaming
about. During my family practice residency I started—
along with Colin Rivers, a dedicated pulmonary doctor—
the Crossover Clinic for the homeless in Richmond,
Virginia. Since I was still spending most of my time learning
to practice medicine, I was able only to get my feet wet at
Crossover. It was not until I finished my training and
decided to move to Memphis that the Church Health
Center was ready to be born.

Eighteen exciting yet awful months passed by from the
time I arrived in Memphis to the Clinic's opening day. I
arrived in Memphis not knowing a soul. I am thankful
that, Frank McRae, along with Michael McLain, a religion
professor at a Memphis college, took me under his wing
and helped me begin to tell people of my dream.

Most people I talked to could see the need for the church's
involvement in health care for the working poor, or at least
they were in some way moved by my enthusiasm. It was not
until I chose the site of the center that opposition started to
arise. When I approached Methodist Hospital for help, a
few doctors balked at the reasons I gave when asking for a
financial gift from the hospital. In time, however, all of these
doctors became regular volunteers for the center. The major

source of opposition came from the neighborhood that is located just east of our original building.

Before we could begin renovating the house, a special use permit was required from the city council. Naively, I thought that would just be a formality. The rules required that all the neighbors of the building be notified of our intentions to change the building from a boarding house to a health care clinic. The notices went out, and just before the deadline for submitting objections, one objection arrived from the nearby neighborhood association.

The building is located in Memphis's first suburb. The houses were built around the turn of the century. To the east, the homes have all been renovated, making the neighborhood one of the nicest in Memphis. To the west, however, urban redevelopment has not yet happened and still seems a long way off. We are just on the edge of the dividing line between gentrification and inner city. Our building sits on the side of inner city.

The families that live in this transition zone remained hopeful that the neighborhood could come back again. I, too, saw the potential and wanted to do what it took to restore the Randolph House to its original beauty. But some of our neighbors were afraid of what our clinic might do to their community.

A neighborhood meeting was called so that I could tell the residents of my dream. It was the first time I ever spoke to such a hostile audience. Previous audiences had patted me on the back and told me how noble my ideas were. Instead of comparing me to Albert Schweitzer, tonight people were picturing me as Atilla the Hun! One man stood up and announced the fears of many. "We all know what will happen," he said. "Young bucks will drop their mothers off and go thieving through the neighborhood." I could feel anger welling up inside me. At that moment they could not understand me, and I surely did not understand them.

After two hours of debate, a vote was taken whether to oppose formally our petition for a special use permit. There were only nine votes cast in our favor. I was crushed. How could this be happening? Could these people end the dream of half my life?

Fortunately, my friends reminded me that this was not the vote that counted. That would come in two weeks at the city council. During that time I took a crash course in local politics. I tried to explain to every city council person how the Church Health Center would help the neighborhood, not hurt it. I had no idea how I was doing. I had never done anything like this before and never dreamed I would have to. I was a doctor. I was a minister. I was not a politician. No one ever told me that providing health care to the poor in the name of the church would require a political battle. "Please, God, help them to make a wise decision," was my prayer every night as I went to bed but not to sleep.

When the day came for the vote, I could not eat. I was not merely anxious—I could feel my heart racing all day. Ann Langston, my new friend, a believer in our mission, and a brilliant attorney, agreed to speak for us before the city council. There is no telling what I would say or how emotional I would be if I were to speak. This was not the time for me to preach a sermon, even though I was ready to do so.

Ann, Frank, Zeno, and I, along with a few others, walked into the council chamber together as our question drew near on the agenda. The room was packed with people opposing our request. I was in shock.

Ann spoke in a calm, logical, measured manner. It was the first time I had heard her argue a case, and from that moment I knew I would always want her on my side. She explained eloquently the benefit the Church Health Center would bring to the city. A city councilwoman quickly interrupted her, however, and asked, "Have you explored any other locations?"

"Yes, ma'am, we have, and we believe this is the best that is available."

The city councilwoman responded, "Well, I don't want it in my neighborhood." She lived almost two miles from our site, quite a distance from our project. I felt my stomach turn over, and I could no longer pay attention to the discussion.

Finally, after almost three hours, it came time to vote. I held my breath and looked straight ahead.

"All in favor say, 'Aye.' Those opposed say, 'No,'" announced the council chair.

"Aye," "Aye," "Aye," "No," "Aye," "Aye," "Aye." It passed. I had permission to get started.

It was a bittersweet victory. I had been given permission to begin a ministry of health care for the working poor in what is historically the poorest major city in America. However, there were those who understandably doubted my intentions and my dream. After all, I was a stranger to Memphis, and few really believed the dream would work. Many people had promised similar programs in the past; I would not have been the first to fail to fulfill promises.

Fortunately, this has not been the case. On the first day
the Church Health Center was open, we treated twelve
patients. We now care for more than 30,000 patients with
30,000 patient visits a year. There are more than 400
physician volunteers with hundreds more nurses, dentists,
optometrists, and nonprofessional volunteers. We have a
paid staff of 150 and are financially supported by the
more than 200 congregations throughout the city. But the
success of the Church Health Center is not told by the
numbers of people who have experienced it, but by the
stories of individuals whose lives have been touched,
including mine, by what goes on inside its walls. This
book tells the stories of a handful of people I have met by
being their physician at the Church Health Center. Each
story stands alone, yet together they weave the fabric
which is a remarkable source of hope and healing for
staff, volunteers, patients, and me. Fourteen years ago
when the city council gave us the go-ahead to begin, I did
not know how the people I would meet as patients would
transform my life. The following stories are an attempt to
reveal my story while telling theirs. In the process of
telling what happened, I have seen clearly how one's
attempt to live a faithful life is shaped not solely by what
he believes but equally by what he does and whom he
spends his life seeking to serve. For me, at least, this way
of living has shaped who I am.

"Ain't You My Doctor?"

Zachius

I saw him walk through the front door as I was coming down the steps from my office. I could tell he was in his mid-fifties. He was tall, 6 feet 2 inches or so, with a gentle but worn face. He caught my eye because he took his hat off when he came through the door. He quickly sized up the office, then limped over to Kim at the reception desk. I knew I would see him in a few minutes, but he had already attracted my attention.

When I walked in the door to the exam room a few minutes later, he stood up to greet me. Softly, he said, "My name is Zachius."

It is an unusual name, so I asked him where it came from. "My mother found it in the Bible," he said. We talked for a few more minutes, then turned to his reason for coming to see me. His hip was hurting and causing him to limp.

I took an X-ray of his hip and found it to have severe changes from degenerative joint disease (commonly referred to as arthritis). His problem was severe enough that I thought he would probably need a hip replacement in the future. But for now we could help him only with pain medicine and advice on how to care for his worn-out hip.

"What kind of work do you do?" I asked.

"I work out of the labor pool."

I was curious. "How do you get jobs?"

"Well, every morning, you just show up about six o'clock, and the bosses pick the ones they want to work for the day. Then they usually take you out east. You do your job, and you get paid at the end of the day. Then you come back and start all over the next day. They usually pick me because they know I'll work hard."

I had little doubt of that, but I could not understand why he could not get a steady, full-time job. I asked, "Why don't you get a regular job?"

Zachius hemmed and hawed, then said, "This just works out better."

My next question was another one I had honed over the years.

"Who do you live with?" I have learned that if I ask, "Where do you live?" I get all kinds of responses from "in Memphis" to "down yonder" to "on Third Street." None of these answers helps me get a feel for a person's living situation, but "Who do you live with?" usually tells me their family status and the type of living quarters they are in.

"I stay here and there," he said, the classic answer of someone who is homeless.

Why should Zachius be homeless? He was smart. He was likable. He was willing to work hard. There could be only one explanation.

"How much alcohol do you drink, Zachius?"

"I don't drink every day, but I have a beer every now and then."

I knew then that Zachius was a binge drinker and had trouble holding a job when he was drinking. Yet, in talking with Zachius I was increasingly drawn by his kind demeanor and gentle ways. I wanted to help him in any way I could, but knew I was limited in what I could do for his hip.

Then I noticed that the shoes he was wearing were completely worn out. I asked him, "How long has it been since you've had a new pair of shoes?"

"Oh, it's been a while. My size is hard to find."

"Well," I said, "have you looked at the clothes closets of any of the churches?"

He could tell that my intentions were good and said, "I've looked, but I can't ever find anything that fits."

I then looked closer at his feet. They were very large! "What size shoe do you wear?" I asked.

"17 EEE," he said matter-of-factly.

I had nothing else to say about his shoes. I wished him well, gave him medicine for his hip, and asked him to return in a month.

That afternoon I remembered Barry Lichterman, a new friend who owned a shoe company. I called him and told him about Zachius. He listened sympathetically and was eager to help. When he asked what size shoes Zachius needed, I responded, "17 EEE." There was silence on the phone.

"We don't carry a shoe that large, but I'll see what I can do," Barry answered.

A couple of weeks went by, and I did not hear back from Barry. I was worried that he had forgotten. Then one day I heard his voice in the waiting room asking Kim if he could see me for a minute. I rushed out to meet him and instantly noticed that he had a shoe box under his arm.

"Oh, Barry, this is so kind of you!" I exclaimed.

"Well, you might want to wait a minute before you say that. This was all I could find."

I took him back into the laboratory, and he gave me the box of shoes. When I opened the box I was stunned. In my hands I held a brand new pair of black, patent leather shoes, shined to such a sparkle that I could see myself in them. Not exactly the best shoes for doing manual labor.

Barry and I both realized the limitation of the shoes, but it was extremely kind on his part. I couldn't wait to give them to Zachius.

When Zachius returned in two weeks, his hip was a little better, but his shoes were the same. After I finished his medical visit, I asked him to wait in the exam room. I went to get the shoes and when I returned, I handed them to him. He opened the box immediately. I could see his eyes light up, and he began to put them on. I started making apologies: "Zachius, I know they are not exactly work boots. Are you sure they will be okay?"

He tried to reassure me.

"They'll do just fine. They fit real good."

When he finished lacing up the shoes, he placed his old, worn-out tennis shoes back in the box, wrapped them up with the tissue paper, and put the box under his arm. There was no question that he looked odd wearing his dress shoes and overalls, but he was smiling from ear to ear. I told him I'd see him soon, and he thanked me one more time.

A few weeks later Barry returned with another box of shoes, this time a real pair of work boots. The next time I saw Zachius I gave them to him. By then, the shine on the black patent leather was long gone. Those shoes were not built for life on the street, but they had done well for a while.

From that point on I would see Zachius sporadically. He would come to have an acute illness treated. Then I might not see him for eight to ten months. An encounter with him that I will never forget did not even occur at the health center.

For about six months I lived in a downtown apartment overlooking the Mississippi River. The place had a lovely view, and the river was a constant lure for me. One night I was having trouble sleeping and decided I would walk down by the river until I was able to go back to sleep. I got dressed, went downstairs, crossed the street, and began walking behind the downtown library.

It was a warm summer night, and the full moon was shining on the river. Despite the beauty of the setting, I was still in the downtown of a major city at two o'clock in the morning, walking alone. It was not really safe to do so, and I should have known better. I was not thinking particularly of my safety until I began to sense that I was not alone.

I had stopped to look at the river when I heard someone moving in the shadows. I looked over my right shoulder and noticed a figure coming toward me. I could tell it was a very tall man. The closer he came, the taller he seemed. I felt a lump in my throat. I thought of running but instead decided to stay still and meet my fate. I reached for my wallet and was prepared to hand it over. By now the figure loomed in front of me and appeared to be at least ten feet tall.

As he came out of the shadows, he strained to look at my face. He looked to the right and then to the left and then began to speak.

"Ain't you my doctor?" he said.

Without pausing I shouted back, "Yes, Jesus, I am." It was Zachius!

He proceeded to give me a lecture about how I should not be downtown late at night by myself. I agreed with him and promised never to do it again. Then I went back to my apartment as quickly as I could. I was so thankful that my stranger in the dark turned out to be a friend that I failed to ask anything about him. On the way back I caught myself smiling and feeling proud that the work I do every day was able to turn a fearful situation into one that made me laugh. What a great thing to turn fear into laughter. I wish it were always so easy.

I did not see Zachius again until he appeared one Saturday afternoon at the soup kitchen that my Sunday School class helps run at St. John's church. I had never seen Zachius eat there before and was surprised to see him that day. When he saw me, he gave me a big smile. I went right to him and greeted him. He nodded his head and said, "I wasn't sure you recognized me at first that night downtown." I laughed and pretended that it was just the same as running into an old friend at the mall. I think he knew I had been shaking in my boots.

I asked him why he was eating at the soup kitchen.

"Well, my hip has been giving me a little problem, and I'm having a little trouble doing the work at the labor pool, and my money is a little tight."

"Come see me on Monday, and I'll see what I can do."

Zachius did show up on Monday, and I could tell that his limp was worse than ever. This was confirmed on a new X-ray. He was still a young man for a hip replacement, but there was no question that he needed one. He was reluctant to have it done.

"I think I'll just wait a little while on that, Doc," he said as he headed for the door.

"But Zach (I had learned that's what his friends called him), you can wait on the surgery, but you've got to get off the street. You're too old for that life, and with your bad hip you're just a target to get beaten up."

"I see your point there, Doc. I'll think about it." I knew he really meant, "I'll see you later, but nothing is going to change."

And nothing did change for a couple of years. I saw Zachius only once or twice in that time period and then one day he appeared for an appointment out of the shadows just like the night downtown. As I began talking to him, I noticed he was carrying a Bible.

"Doctor Morris, I want you to know that I've stopped drinking, and I've found religion." He looked at me and smiled. "Everything's going to work out fine for me now." He was still smiling.

"I'm so glad to hear that, Zachius. Are you still on the street?"

"No, my aunt has let me come back to live with her, and I've applied to live in the high rise. I need your help to fill out this form, if you don't mind."

I was glad to fill out his form, but his news seemed too good to be true. It was the first of December when Zachius told me how his life had changed.

Every year at Thanksgiving and Christmas, Sunday School classes from various churches come to us, offering to provide dinners, Christmas presents, and food for a handful of our patients. While I greatly appreciate the kindness of those gifts, I cannot help but remember a story I once heard former President Jimmy Carter tell.

President Carter was talking about the role of the church in social issues. He used his own Sunday School class as an example. He said,

"Every year at Thanksgiving my Sunday School class decides to do something for a poor family, and every year the situation is the same. We look around at each other and ask, 'Does anyone know a family who needs our help?' There is usually silence. Then someone will say, 'Let's go down to the welfare office and ask them for a recommendation.' And that is what we do. Say what you will about the government, at least the government knows where the poor live. All too often, the church doesn't even know that."

I am always glad when Sunday School classes turn to us to help match them up with families in need because I believe President Carter would be pleased to know that the church is beginning to do better at knowing where the poor live.

This particular December we were given a dozen turkeys and various presents we were allowed to give out ourselves.

I decided I would find Zachius's aunt's house and take a turkey and present to him.

I looked on the map for the address he had given us. It was in a part of town where I had never been. Late that afternoon it began to rain and as the evening went on, it rained harder and harder. It was about six o'clock before I left the health center. It was dark and turning cold. I had a little trouble reading the street signs because of the rain, but I found my way without too much difficulty.

It was a winding route to get to the house, and with every turn the houses were smaller and in worse condition. I eventually came to the address I had written on a card. It was what is known as a shotgun house—a three-room house, with each room behind the other, lined up perpendicular to the street so that a shotgun blast through the front door would go through every room without hitting a wall.

With my coat pulled over my head, the turkey under one arm, and the present under the other, I ran through the rain from the car to the porch. I could not tell whether anyone was at home. It seemed dark inside the house, but I went ahead and knocked on the door. In just a moment an elderly woman, small and frail, opened the door. She did not seem all that surprised to see me.

"Hello, ma'am, I'm Doctor Scott Morris from the Church Health Center. Does Zachius McMichael live here?"

She looked me over quickly, sizing me up. I must not have seemed a threat because she smiled at me and said, "Won't you come in?"

I smiled back, thanked her, and stepped across the threshold into her living room.

It took a moment for my eyes to adjust. The only light in the room was coming from a light bulb hanging down from the center of the room. I could tell the room was clean, but there was almost no furniture to speak of. Two wooden framed chairs with plastic seats, the kind I remember from the sixies, and an old colonial-looking couch, which was well-worn in the seat, were all there was.

"Can I take your coat, Doctor? It's a terrible night out there."

I thanked her and handed over my coat after setting the turkey on one of the chairs.

She called to the back room, "Zach, there is someone to see you."

In a few moments I could see Zachius walking through the doorway. Because of the lack of light, I could only make out his outline, just like the night downtown by the river. Only this time I knew it was him.

He limped into the room, but stopped in his tracks when he saw it was me. He broke out into a broad smile.

"Land sakes, what can I do for you?"

I was taken aback. Not, "What are you doing here?" but, "What can I do for you?" I didn't really know what to say to him. I had not thought out a speech. I had just come.

I went over and picked up the turkey and the present. I didn't know what was inside the gift; the card on the box only read, "For a man." I told him, "Some people gave the Center a few turkeys, and I thought you and your aunt might like one."

He held out his hand, and I gave it to him.

"Thank you, we'd be glad to accept it."

I was stuck on what to say next. "How's your hip doing?" I muttered.

"It bothers me a bit when it rains like this, but it's not doing too bad."

There was really no small talk we could exchange with each other. I was beginning to feel awkward when his aunt said, "Zach, is this your doctor? Well, I'll be! You've got yourself a good-looking doctor."

We all laughed, and I made my way to the door. They both thanked me again.

As I was about to leave, Zachius said, "Hold on a minute," and he went to the back room. He came back with a sheet of plastic to put over my head so I wouldn't get wet.

"Take care, Doc. I'll be by to see you soon."

"So long, Zachius. Have a good Christmas."

"I will now," he said.

I ran to my car, got in, and drove away. I did not turn on the radio as I usually do. I just drove through the rain with only the sound of the windshield wipers. I was not sure what to make of what happened. I knew that I had not done anything particularly profound, but I felt a calm and peace that I have not experienced very often. There was no sense that there was anything left to do—I had already done it. At least for the drive home, my mind was content to think only about Zachius and his aunt. The feeling of contentment was ever so pleasant.

Since that night, I have continued to see Zachius off and on. He now lives in the "high rise" and is on disability for his hip. He's still thinking about having the surgery, but for now he is willing to continue to limp along. At least he is off the street.

I have never talked to him about that Christmas visit, but I know that when he sees me, he, too, feels a bond that is more than either one of us can explain. We are both willing to let it be a mystery.

"God is Watching Out for Me"

Annie

"Hello, Mrs. Jones. I'm Doctor Morris. What can I do for you today?"

It took me years to come up with that opening line. I like it because it lets patients know I am there to help them and it quickly gets us to the reason they have come to the doctor. But I found that this opening line does not always work, nor should it.

"My name is Annie," Mrs. Jones replied. "I'm here because my boss lady told me to come."

I felt an instant rapport with Mrs. Jones. Like many of the African-American women I had treated, she worked as a housekeeper—long hours for little pay. She hardly ever complained. She had grown up in rural Mississippi and had picked cotton as a child. During her life she had had little medical care except from someone called a "root doctor."

I had never heard of root doctors until I came to Memphis, but in rural Mississippi, even today, they play a role similar to that of the nyanga in Zimbabwe. They are trusted and respected people, handing out folk remedies for a small price. Often the "medicine" comes from boiling roots either dug up by the patient or sold by the root doctor. Today, the advice is more in the form of cod liver oil, Dr. Tishner's cough syrup, or, in the case of a child's ear infection, sweet oil. Root doctors are not as common as they once were, but they are still around in one form or another.

Mrs. Jones had worked as a housekeeper for the same family for more than thirty years. She had gotten married in 1950, left Mississippi, and come to Memphis. Her husband did odd jobs here and there but was mostly dependent on her to pay the bills. She had three children, now all grown. One had left Memphis and gone to Chicago. The other two, both with drug problems, were still in town. The younger daughter had given her own child to Mrs. Jones to take care of, and they lived in subsidized housing in a rough part of town.

"Mrs. Jones, do you have any medical problems that you know about?" I asked her.

"Are you talking to me?"

"Yes, ma'am."

"My name is Annie, Doctor Morris."

My attempt to treat her as my equal was being thwarted, or so I thought.

"Well, Annie, have you ever been told that you have any medical problems?"

"The doctor once said my blood was high and that I had sugar problems, Doctor Scott. Is it okay if I call you that?" It seemed we were back on even terms.

"Yes, ma'am."

Annie did indeed have hypertension and diabetes, both of which I began to treat that day. I asked her to come back in a couple of weeks so that I could see how she was doing.

On her return visit, I noticed she was wearing the same high-collared dress she had worn during the first visit. The fabric was a pale blue, flowered print. She wore her graying hair up, giving her a certain dignity. She was a tall woman, very thin but strong, both in body and in character. When I had examined her arms and legs, I noticed she was very muscular. I was sure she was stronger than me. She probably did more manual work in a week than I did in a year.

When Annie returned, both her blood pressure and diabetes were much improved, so I had time to learn more about her. She told me about the folks she worked for, an old Memphis family who treated her kindly. I quickly learned, however, that her family life was not pleasant. Her husband, John, abused her regularly. He drank heavily every night and often beat her.

"He never really hurts me, Doctor Scott, but I worry he may do something to the baby," she said referring to her granddaughter. "Please don't tell him any of this when you see him," she said.

"I won't Annie, but I hope I never meet him." I was starting to feel a great deal of anger toward this man I had never met.

"Well, I think he is your next patient. I liked you so much I talked him into coming here, too."

She was right. In the next examining room was a big, burly man with one eye scarred over from a childhood injury. He stood up when I walked in, but it was all I could do to shake his hand and ask him what I could do for him. While we talked, he kept saying, "Yes, sir." I wanted to stay aloof, and I could not get out of the room fast enough. Unfortunately, he too had hypertension, so I would have to continue to see him on a regular basis.

Over the next year, I saw Annie once every one or two months. She would often come for small, uncomplicated illnesses, but I enjoyed getting to know her better. The next year while doing a routine breast exam, I noticed a firmness in her left breast that should not have been there.

"Annie, have you felt this before?"

"No, Doctor Scott, but I don't ever know what I'm feeling when I feel around there."

I arranged for her to have a mammogram the next day, and my worst fear was true. She had breast cancer. It was my job to tell her the diagnosis. We sat in the smallest of our three examining rooms. Once again she wore her blue flowered dress. She sat with her back straight and her eyes toward me. I took her by the hand and said, "Annie, I'm afraid that little place in your breast is breast cancer. I think you will need surgery to remove it, but I intend to get you the best care Memphis has to offer."

"Well, Doctor Scott," she said, "I know that you and the Lord will take care of me. Whatever you say, I'll do. Jesus is watching out over you, and he won't lead you wrong."

I tried to reassure her; then I left the room to arrange for her to see the surgeon. Her words had given me both a sadness and a sense of affirmation that I had seldom felt before.

The next week I went to see her at the hospital early in the morning before she was taken to surgery. The surgery went well, but the cancer had already spread to almost all of her lymph nodes, a very bad sign.

When I visited her in her room after her surgery, she was her same stoic self, but, for the first time, she looked somewhat frail. She was in her room all alone—no family, no friends, just her. She was reading the Bible when I walked in.

"I knew you would come," she said.

"Everything's going to be all right, Annie," I tried to comfort her.

"I know. God is watching out for me."

Six weeks after the operation, she visited me in the office. She seemed fully recovered.

"Don't you want to see where they took off my tit?" she asked nonchalantly.

"Yes, ma'am. I'd like to make sure it is healing well."

She quickly dropped her blouse so that both her left chest wall and her right breast were exposed. There was no sense of immodesty. She simply wanted me to see how she was doing. She trusted me.

The incision was healing well, and her blood pressure and diabetes were doing okay, so we agreed to go back to our routine of visits every other month. Yet when I saw her next, I knew all was not well with Annie.

"John says I'm only half a woman so he's gone and found him a girlfriend."

I was outraged. Annie and I agreed that she should talk to Beth, our pastoral counselor. She could stand all the abuse and drinking, but this was too much. For the first time in front of me, she began to cry. There was nothing for me to do but quietly hold her hand.

I saw John a few months later.

"Has anything new happened, John?" I asked obliquely.

"No, everything's fine, Doctor Scott. Everything's fine," he answered.

Seeing Beth apparently helped Annie. During the next several visits she seemed to have returned to her former way of coping with her life's circumstances. Then one day she told me, "John's packed his bags and gone to live with his girlfriend. There's just me and Judy, my grandbaby, left." Her eyes welled with tears.

Over the next six months Annie adjusted fairly well to living alone and taking care of her grandchild on her own. She was resigned to her fate, but she kept believing that God would provide for her. She went to church every time the doors were open, singing in the choir for the first time in her life.

Just as things seemed to be getting better, however, Annie's world exploded. She came to me with a sore throat that would not go away. When I looked in her mouth, I saw she had an obvious case of thrush, a fungus infection which children sometimes get and adults who are immuno-compromised may develop. Why would this be happening to Annie?

Why was her immune system not functioning properly? She was not taking chemotherapy for the cancer. I decided to check her HIV status. She was positive. Annie had AIDS.

I immediately checked John also, who, no surprise, was also positive. After questioning him, he admitted to a long history of intravenous drug use.

"Do you think, Doctor Scott, that's how I got it, or do you think Annie gave it to me?"

"Mr. Jones, call me Doctor Morris. And, yes, I think you got it from the drugs."

When I told Annie, her only concern was whether John would be okay. I tried to tell her, "Annie, I'm not worried about John, we need to take care of you."

But she insisted, "I know he's not been the best of husbands, but I'm still his wife, and I'm supposed to look out for him."

And that's what happened. After John's girlfriend found out about John's HIV infection, she quickly sent him packing. He immediately ran back to Annie. Without much resistance, she let him back into the apartment.

"Annie, I can't understand why you would let him back," I said.

"I know you are looking out for me, Doctor Scott, but he needs someone to take care of him. I'm all he has."

For a short while things went okay for Annie. She took her AIDS medicines regularly and continued to see me for her blood pressure and diabetes. Then one day she fell in the bathtub and broke her right femur—the bone in her thigh. Unfortunately, it did not break from the force of the fall but because the breast cancer had spread to the bone. Cancer was also found in her spine.

The next time I saw her, she was sitting in a wheelchair wearing her favorite blue dress.

"How are you doing, Annie?"

"I'm doing pretty well. God is looking out for me."

She had developed a peace about her that transcended the circumstances of her life. She had a sense of calm that was contagious, and her presence was just as pleasant as ever.

Until the fall she had continued to work as much as possible, and her "family" was understanding of her situation. But after she broke her leg, she had to stop working. I asked Beth to help her get any assistance she could, but there was little available for Annie other than Medicaid. In talking with Beth, Annie asked for an electric fan. It was summer and her apartment was not air-conditioned. The one fan she did have was broken.

The next week, I was preaching at a conference in eastern Tennessee and told Annie's story in my sermon. After the service was over, a stranger gave me a check for $500.00 to buy Annie an air conditioner.

"Oh my, this is more than anybody has ever done for me except my Jesus," said Annie when Beth gave her the check. "But all I need is a fan. I'd be thankful for a fan, but please take the rest of the money and give it to someone who needs it more than me."

Later Beth asked me what she should do. I thought for a moment, then said, "Buy her a fan. Help someone else with the rest of the money."

From that point on, Annie slowly went downhill. Every time I saw her in the office, she had lost more weight. Her fractured leg never completely healed. Nevertheless she continued to care for John and Judy, although I'm not sure how she did it. I arranged for a home health aide to visit her at home three days a week, a gesture she seemed to appreciate. It became difficult for her to bathe herself, and she had trouble cooking dinner.

Her apartment was on the second floor, and it was an ordeal for her to get up and down the stairs, but she managed. Seeing her waste away, I broached the subject I knew she did not want to hear.

"Annie, maybe you would do better if you moved into a nursing home. Then someone could take care of you day and night."

She looked at me sternly. "Doctor Scott, who would take care of John? I know you're trying to help, but Jesus will watch out for me."

There was no point in pressing the suggestion. I let it drop and tried to think of ways to make her life at home more comfortable.

Several weeks later I got a call from a woman who insisted on talking to me and no one else. She identified herself only as Vera. "Mamma told me to call you. Her name is Annie Jones. She passed last night."

I felt a lump in my throat. "What happened?"

"My father just found her in the bed this morning. She told me to call you when the time came. Thank you for your help."

She hung up. That was all.

I realized Annie was the first patient whom I had gotten to know well over a long period of time and who then died. She was a remarkable woman. She was not profound in her thinking, but she had a depth about her you don't see every day. Her faith was unshakable, something I admired then and still do. At every turn she knew that her Jesus was watching out for her. She also had a belief in marriage that was admirable. Despite John's endless abuse, she never once wavered in her responsibility as she saw it to take care of him. That same commitment and ethic of responsibility allowed her to raise her granddaughter while her daughter fed her drug habit. Annie never complained about this unasked-for task. Judy would often come with her to see me, and while Annie would bemoan the fact that she did not know anymore how to look after a child, she was always willing to face the task.

Annie was fiercely loyal to me. The nurses knew that if Annie called, she would not be satisfied until she knew that the nurse had talked directly to me. I did not have any more special knowledge than any other doctor, but that was not the point with Annie. She trusted me, and that gave her confidence in me. She knew I had her best interest at heart. It wasn't my brain she cared about; it was my faithfulness to her that mattered. She knew that I was not going to abandon her.

After she died, I did not see John for several years. Then out of the blue, he showed up one afternoon. He came with his daughter, Vera.

"Doctor Scott," he began, "they tell me that I have AIDS, but I don't believe it. You've always been my doctor, and I know I can trust you to tell me the truth. That's not what I have, is it?"

I looked at him at first with anger, remembering how horribly he had treated Annie; then slowly I tried to act toward him the way I knew she would want me to. She died believing it was her responsibility to care for John, and out of respect for her I felt compelled to show him a kindness it was hard to feel.

"John, I know it's hard to believe, but you do have AIDS. But I'll stick with you and help you fight it to the end."

He probably never really listened to anything I said, but it didn't matter. I was doing it for Annie.

When John died a couple of months later, I felt a sense of closure to my relationship with Annie. And after a while I did not think of Annie in any conscious sense.

Then, six years after her death, her memory and her strength of presence suddenly came back to me. I walked into an examination room one afternoon, and a young woman said to me, "I bet you don't remember me."

She did not look familiar, so I said, "Help me with your name."

"I'm Judy, Annie Jones's granddaughter. She always told me if I was ever in trouble, I could come to you."

And so, my relationship with Annie goes on and, I know now, will continue in one way or another for the rest of my life. It is amazing to me that Annie has touched my life in such a profound way, but she has. I continue to feel her presence and influence in my daily existence. I keep hoping that I can make some of her strengths—trust, faithfulness, simplicity, responsibility—a part of me as well. To remember her inspires me to try, but I know I still have much to learn.

Taking Care of Merilyn's Little Fellow

Kevin

"I know I don't have an appointment, but I'm sick. Isn't this a doctor's office? Don't you take care of sick people? That's why I'm here. I know the doctor will want to see me. I'll just go talk to him."

Kevin strolled, or rather seemed to prance, across the waiting room and entered the examining room area. I was standing at the nurses' station talking on the phone when I first saw him. He was about six feet tall and had short blond hair and a baby face. He was thin but fairly muscular. I remember he wore dark blue eyeliner, bright red lipstick, and pink rouge. He had on a short denim skirt that came to the middle of his thigh. The clogs he was wearing announced his presence long before he came into view.

"Excuse me. Are you the doctor? I need to see you," he said looking at me.

"I'll be with you in a minute," I said, as I took the telephone receiver away from my ear.

"I really need to see you," he continued without hesitating. He paused for a brief, seemingly feigned cough. "I'm about to die. Really, I am."

By this time, Merilyn, the nurse, had taken him by the arm and was leading him back to the waiting room. She then returned and asked, "What do you want to do?"

I paused, then said, "I guess we'll see him."

As I was talking to the next patient, I could hear Kevin out in the hall making some sort of commotion. Merilyn knocked on the door and asked if I could see him next. I decided that was probably a good idea.

As I entered the examining room, Kevin was rummaging through the medical supplies. When he saw me, he abruptly stopped and ran over to the examining table and sat down. I began asking him about his problem.

"I have this cough, and I need some medicine," he said politely.

It was only then that I noticed that each of his fingernails and toenails was painted a different color and that he wore multiple rings in his right ear. This was long before men began wearing earrings. I also noticed that his clothes were dirty, and he reeked of body odor.

"When was the last time you had a bath?" I asked.

"I dunno, not too long ago," he responded.

"Where are you living?"

"Here and there."

I knew this meant he was homeless.

"Do you have family in Memphis?"

"Yeah, but they don't understand me. They think I'm some kind of freak."

"Do you have a place to stay tonight?"

"I'll find someplace."

"Do you know about the shelters downtown?"

"Yeah, but people beat me up when I go down there," he laughed heartily.

As calmly as I was talking to Kevin, I had never really met anyone like him. He was clearly a cross-dresser—living the life of a woman but obviously fully aware he was a man. I had to admit that I did not know how to take him seriously. I decided to just treat his symptoms and go on.

"Wait here and the nurse will bring you your medicine," I explained. "I hope you feel better soon."

I left the room and told Merilyn what medicine he needed. At the time I had no idea what sort of bond would be formed as a result of this chance encounter between Merilyn and Kevin.

I had first met Merilyn when I worked for the public health department and was trying to raise funds for the Church Health Center opening. Merilyn, an African American, was the well-child nurse and worked at the other end of the hall at the health clinic. Whenever the pediatrician was gone, she would come to me with her questions because she knew I was a family practitioner.

I liked her immediately. She was kind and had a gentle, warm smile. She grew up on a farm in rural Mississippi. Her parents were hard-working but uneducated folks who managed to raise their family and put three children through college. Merilyn wanted the best education available, so despite the school's history of prejudice she went without hesitation to nursing school at the University of Mississippi.

When the Church Health Center first opened, I coaxed Merilyn into volunteering for us. As soon as we needed another nurse, she was my first choice. She was eager to accept the challenge and immediately fit into the mission of the Center. That first day when she met Kevin, she treated him with the kindness that her mother had taught her to show to everyone—a kindness that Kevin would never forget.

I had all but forgotten about Kevin when several weeks later, he burst through the door, shouting, "I need to see the doctor. I know I'm about to die."

Kim, the receptionist, again tried to explain to him that he needed an appointment, but he was oblivious to everything she said.

Once again I opted to see him. However, by the time I got to him, he really had no complaint of any illness. He was dressed very much as before, and his flamboyance was every bit as dramatic.

"Kevin, are you still living on the street?" I asked.

"Where else would I live?" he quipped. "Is Merilyn here? Tell her I need to speak to her."

"What about, Kevin?"

"It's very important."

I told him that she had stepped out for a moment.

"Well, okay," he said, sounding most disappointed. "Tell her I really need to talk to her."

Hoping that I had distracted him from Merilyn, I led him to the waiting room. Then he spotted her at the end of the hall. With all the flair of a queen from Manhattan, Kevin flew down the hall, hugged Merilyn, and kissed her on the cheek. "I am so glad to see you!" he exclaimed.

Merilyn had a look of absolute shock on her face, but she quickly composed herself and said, "I'm glad to see you, too, Kevin. How are you doing?"

At once he began to tell her all that was on his mind. I questioned Merilyn with my expression as to whether she needed help. But she shook her head at me, indicating she had things under control.

I went on to see the next patient, but when I came back into the hall, Merilyn was busily going about her job with Kevin trailing behind her. After a few more minutes, however, she managed to show him to the door.

From that point on, at least once a week for the next six months, Kevin would make an appearance. Ostensibly his visits were to see the doctor, but usually he was satisfied if he got to talk to Merilyn even for a few minutes. I sometimes tried to talk with him about finding a permanent home, but he would only laugh and say, "No one wants a pretty boy like me."

One day Kevin was out in the waiting room, but he was not his usual overbearing self. He was subdued. His eye was blackened and his face swollen. Someone had beaten him up.

While I saw several other patients, I was aware that Kevin was waiting. Because it was so quiet, I kept checking to see whether he had left. Every time I looked out in the waiting room, I could see he was still there. He sat quietly, looking down at the floor.

By the time I opened the door to his exam room, Merilyn had already begun to clean his wounds. In a kind, almost motherly way, she stroked his face and patted his back. This seemed to bring him back to life, and he began his usual chatter.

"What happened to you, Kevin?" I asked.

"I fell down and hit my face."

When I looked at him closely, I could tell that not only was his face swollen, but his arms were bruised. As I touched his chest, he jumped back in pain.

"Ouch, that hurts! Don't you know you're supposed to help me, not hurt me?" he exclaimed.

"Sorry, Kevin. Who beat you?"

"I'm okay, I just fell down." He seemed a little withdrawn.

"Kevin, if someone hurt you, we should call the police," I suggested naively.

He glanced at me quickly and replied, "I don't think the police are going to help me." I paused for a moment, then acknowledged sadly that he was probably right. He had turned to us because he knew we would at least take his injuries seriously.

"I wish it weren't that way, Kevin," was all I could say.

Fortunately his injuries were not too serious and would heal fairly quickly. It was not the first time this had happened, so he knew that in time he would be better. There was little else I could do except tell him that Merilyn would be in shortly to finish cleaning up his wounds. When I left the room, she was waiting outside for me to come out.

I looked at her and asked, "Do you mind cleaning Kevin up a little more?"

"I've got to take care of my little sweetie," she replied. She accepted the charge without hesitation.

While I was talking to the next patient, I heard Kevin's voice crying out above all else—bantering, jabbering away. He was resilient; he was himself again, or at least not so broken as when he had first walked through our door.

Over the next few months we continued to see Kevin off and on. Hearing his voice several times a week became commonplace. On a couple of occasions we went a week without seeing him, and I would say to Merilyn, "I wonder where Kevin is."

"I don't know. I need to check on my little fellow."

On one occasion, he had been in jail for solicitation. Other times we just never knew. And then, without warning, we never saw him again.

Every day I expected to hear Kevin coming through the door. Although at times he was an incredible bother, I felt very comfortable with him being around. Even though Kevin had refused to grant me access to anything more than his act, his facade, I found I respected and liked him. I did know, however, what I saw was all I would get from Kevin.

What I saw in Kevin was more than I could understand. I wondered why someone would put himself through such torture. What possible benefit could there be? But there was something about Kevin's openness and trusting behavior that made me feel drawn to him. He seemed so needy; yet when I drew near to him, he was inclined to take all I had to give until I cried out, "Enough!"

After Kevin's last visit, from time to time I would ask Merilyn, "What do you think has happened to Kevin?"

She would always say in a halfway laughing but sincere voice, "I don't know. I'm a little worried about the little fellow."

As time went on, I put Kevin out of my mind. There were new patients every day. I concentrated on them while my concern for Kevin faded. Then one day, almost five years after his last visit, Merilyn said to me, "Guess who called me last night?"

"I don't know."

"Kevin," she said proudly.

I was stunned. "Merilyn, how did he get your phone number?"

She grinned sheepishly. "I gave it to him. Back when he was coming to see us, he would call me from time to time. I told him it was okay to call if he ever needed me."

"Well?" I looked at her. "What did he say? Where is he?"

"He's been living in San Francisco for the last few years. He feels more accepted out there. There are more people like him."

"So why did he call you?" I asked.

"He's worried that he might have AIDS and wanted to talk to someone, so he called me. He wanted to apologize for when he used to come see us. He said that was back when he thought he was Tina Turner, but he's gotten over that now."

"Is that all?" I asked.

"He went on for a while. It was good to talk to my little fellow again. He told me about San Francisco and his life there. He seems to be doing a lot better. But he was a little sad." I could tell that Merilyn was moved by the fact that Kevin had chosen to call her when he was down and needed a real friend.

That was the last time we heard from Kevin. He never called Merilyn again. From time to time I think of him. I would not be surprised if he walked in one day and demanded to be seen. But mostly I have tried to learn from Merilyn about the ways one cares for someone who is different from oneself.

We often talk about compassion and kindness, but Merilyn's acts of gentleness and tenderness with Kevin stick in my mind as the way it should be. She never did anything dramatic for him, but when this lost child of God needed human contact with someone who would care about him and care for him, it was Merilyn he called. She never judged his behavior; instead she reached out to soothe his wounds. What more can be asked of one spirit in caring for another?

The Strength to Live

Phen

When I was a resident physician in Richmond, Virginia, I became friends with a young Cambodian woman named Lelea who worked at night in the hospital's housekeeping department. Often Lelea and I would find ourselves alone, the only people in the corridor at 3:00 A.M., and we would talk. She was always friendly and asked about my dog, Pilgrim. I would ask about her children, who were five, seven, and nine years old. Usually, I was just trying to make pleasant conversation to help pass the time while I waited on an x-ray test to be done on a patient.

One night I asked Lelea, "Why did you come to America?"

She looked away and said, "It's a long story." She began walking away.

"No, really, Lelea, I've got time," I said. "Tell me your story."

She paused for a moment then while looking at the ground, she began talking. "My mother and I left our village with my children after the Khmer Rouge killed my father and husband."

"How did it happen?" I asked, stunned at the response to my casual question.

She hesitated briefly and then continued. "One night they came to our village and made all the men come to the center of our houses. They then lined up the older men, including my father, and shot them one by one. They tied the younger men to a rope and began to lead them away. I ran to the soldier who had my husband and began screaming at him and beating on his chest. He laughed at me and made a joke to his friends.

"He said to me, 'So you want your husband to stay?' I fell to my knees and began pleading with him to let him go free. The soldier then untied my husband, and for a moment I thought they would let him go. Instead he led him over to the well in the center of the village and pushed him into it. Then all the soldiers began throwing rocks down the well onto him. I could hear his screams, but there was nothing I could do. After a few minutes he fell silent, and the soldiers brushed off their hands and walked away.

"The soldier I had pleaded with came up to me as I was crying on the ground and said, 'You can keep him now; he will not be of any use to us anymore.' And then he left with the others.

"Afterwards, my mother and I could not stay in our village any longer. I was in constant fear the soldiers would come back to get my sons. So we went to the refugee camp in Laos. It was hard, but now things are better, even though I miss my home and my husband and father."

I was speechless. I suspected that her life had been difficult, but I could not imagine living through such a horror and having to make a new life in a foreign country.

When the Church Health Center opened, it was not long before we began seeing a variety of refugees who made their way to us, and many of them were from Cambodia. One of the first was Mrs. Nantawong. Her children had come to America about the same time as Lelea, during the reign of terror of the Khmer Rouge.

Mrs. Nantawong had stayed behind because she could not bear to leave all that she had known. She had successfully survived the tumult, but then suddenly at the age of ninety she decided to emigrate to America to be with her children and grandchildren. By the time she arrived, her grandchildren lived in Memphis and owned a Chinese restaurant. The whole family worked together to make the restaurant a success, and they were developing a growing number of faithful patrons.

When Mrs. Nantawong arrived in the United States, the family was honored to have her back with them, but they did not know what to do about her long list of medical complaints. At first she was willing to be treated with only Oriental or Asian medicines, but they offered her little relief, so she relented and came to the Church Health Center.

The first day I saw her, she sat calmly in her seat with her granddaughter at her side. She was small in stature with weather-beaten skin. She was frail and appeared to be ill. It was necessary for me to examine her, so I told the granddaughter, who conveyed my request that she get undressed.

When I returned, she sat on the end of the table, completely nude. Her paper gown was folded nicely on her lap. I had obviously not been clear in my instructions.

After finishing my exam I tried to help her off the table back to the chair so she could get dressed. Before I knew what was happening, Mrs. Nantawong grabbed my neck for support, and I lost my balance and fell down on top of her. I was now lying prone on an exam table with a sick, nude, 90-year-old woman from Cambodia who spoke no English. She and I both began to laugh. We knew nothing about each other and understood each other's culture even less. There was little doubt she had suffered far more than I could ever understand, but for a short moment we were joined together by the absolute absurdity of the moment.

I got up and called for Merilyn's assistance. I stepped out of the room and left Merilyn to aid her in getting dressed. A short time later I returned momentarily to get her chart. When I opened the door, Merilyn was holding Mrs. Nantawong in her arms and, with the gentlest of care, lifting her off the table and onto the floor. It was a lovely moment that has stayed with me for years.

Mrs. Nantawong was in congestive heart failure and needed to be admitted to the hospital. There seemed to be no other alternative. I discussed it with her grandchildren, who agreed with my decision, but they were worried about how she would respond to the hospital environment. I assured them that the hospital staff would take good care of her. Little did I know the challenge she would present to the nursing staff.

Late that night I got a call from the hospital to which I had admitted Mrs. Nantawong.

"Is this Dr. Morris?" a frustrated voice began.

"Yes, is there a problem?"

"That's putting it mildly. You've got to do something about your patient."

"What is going on?" I calmly asked.

"She has pulled out all her IVs and will not let anyone touch her, and now she is sitting in the main hall on the floor in the lotus position chanting. She is disturbing the whole floor. You've got to get her out of here!" The nurse was at her wit's end.

Mrs. Nantawong's adjustment to the hospital environment had proved to be considerably more difficult than I ever imagined. As quickly as I could, I arranged for her to be discharged from the hospital. Everyone was relieved— the nurses, Mrs. Nantawong, and especially her family, who had tried their best to get her to follow the rules of the hospital. It was just too foreign to her.

There are times when a person can be asked to give up more of who she is than she is capable of doing. Apparently Mrs. Nantawong had felt totally compromised by the hospital experience, and the promise of feeling better was not worth turning over her entire sense of dignity and self.

She had already given up her home and her homeland. She could not also give up her sense of autonomy and her identity. I was sorry I had not foreseen what would happen. Fortunately, Mrs. Nantawong's family gave her excellent care and were able to nurse her back to health within a few days.

Several weeks after her adventure in the hospital I went to the family's Chinese restaurant for dinner. As I waited for my meal, I could see Mrs. Nantawong overseeing her family's work as she maintained her place in the kitchen. It was a heartwarming sight.

My experiences with Lelea and Mrs. Nantawong heightened my sensitivity for caring for Cambodian refugees; and during the first few years the Church Health Center was open, we frequently treated Cambodians as they came to Memphis. Many arrived through the refugee resettlement program of Catholic Charities, while others came as their families petitioned to have loved ones come to the United States from refugee camps in Laos and Thailand.

I was always glad to see the Cambodians but was frustrated when no one came with them who could translate Cambodian to English. Fortunately, with each new Cambodian there began to be a familiar figure who came for the sole purpose of translating. His name was Phen Phong. I soon developed an affection for Phen Phong because his help was invaluable, and he was always extremely friendly and kind.

After a few visits he began to understand what information I would want, and as soon as I entered the room he was prepared to give me all of the answers to my questions. At one point of particularly heavy immigration, I saw him almost every day.

On one occasion, I entered the exam room and saw Phen Phong sitting in the patient's chair. I nodded hello to him then looked to meet my new patient only to find no one else present.

Phen Phong smiled and said, "I am your new patient today."

I smiled back. I wanted to help him in any way I could. Although I had felt like I knew him well as a person, I realized that I knew nothing about him.

I sat down and began to talk with him about why he had come to see me. For some reason I remembered my startling conversation with Lelea and had the urge to ask him about his physical symptoms only. I was certain that he too must have a story of horror to tell, and I did not want to intrude. Most of all, I was not sure I wanted to hear such a story. But I did want to get to know him. I tried to lay aside my own anxiety, and I asked, "Tell me why you left Cambodia and came to Memphis."

He responded, "I know you are busy, and it is a long story. I do not wish to take up your time."

"No, Phen Phong, tell me your story," I urged him gently. He seemed grateful that I sincerely wanted to know about him.

He began slowly. "I left Cambodia while the Khmer Rouge were in power. Have you heard of them?"

I flashed back to Lelea's story, "Yes, I know of them and what they did."

Phen Phong continued. "My village is near the border with Vietnam. During the Vietnam War my father helped the Americans when they came through our village. After the war was over and the Khmer Rouge took over the Cambodian government, they came to our village looking for my father. They hated anyone who had sympathy for the West and especially Americans. My father knew they were coming, so he fled his home and left me in charge of our field and our family. I was only sixteen years old at the time. When the soldiers arrived, they questioned everyone about my father until they were convinced that he was gone. Then they came to my home and beat my mother. They then came to my room and dragged me out of my house by my feet. Since I was the oldest son, I was to pay for the sins of my father.

"They marched me with other prisoners across the country until we reached a prison camp. I was lucky they did not kill me on the spot because this is what would have happened had they found my father. Instead, they kept me in a bamboo cell."

I had seen movies about the cruelty of the Khmer Rouge prisons. The movie *The Killing Fields* had won an Academy Award, and I had a vision of it in my mind as Phen Phong spoke. "Tell me about your cell," I asked.

"It was very small," he said. "I could not stand up straight and could not lay down flat. It was only about 4 feet by 4 feet by 4 feet. I could only see the sky out of one corner of the roof. It was more like a cage than a cell."

"How long were you there?" I asked.

"I lived there for four years. They would let me out for a few minutes every two or three days, but that is all. I received one bowl of rice a day. After about a year I became very sick. I could not eat anything, and I had constant diarrhea. I thought I was going to die."

His reason for coming to see me was that he had been told at the blood bank that he had hepatitis and needed to be examined by a doctor. I suspected that it was hepatitis he had while in captivity, for his blood tests did indeed show he had had the virus in the past.

"How did you escape?" I was enthralled by his story.

"One night my guard came to me and opened the

cage. He told me to get out and take off all my clothing. I was afraid I was about to be beaten. He told me to walk forward toward the woods. He had his gun drawn, and I was sure he was about to shoot me. I was not afraid, but I did not want to hear the gun go off, so I put my hands over my ears and walked slowly into the woods. Nothing happened.

"I eventually came to a river. I was not sure what to do. I did not really know where I was but thought I was near the Laotian border. It was dark, but I sensed my chance to be free. I walked into the river and began to float downstream. I climbed on top of a log and floated with it for three days. I was near death when the river came around a bend and I could see a sea of tents. It was a refugee camp. I climbed out onto the river bank and people came down to help me. It turned out it was the same refugee camp that my father had fled to.

"I stayed in the camp for almost two years, but eventually I was granted a visa to go to America. I studied English every day because I knew that my new life would mean everything would be different and I must begin to change. The officials at the camp told me my father had initially gone to Los Angeles, so that is where I wanted to go. But when I arrived, I was told he had left and gone to Memphis, Tennessee. I had never heard of Tennessee, much less Memphis, but here is where I found my father."

It was an incredible story. I doubted whether I could have survived the same ordeal. I asked Phen Phong, "How were you able to live through all you did?"

He did not hesitate to answer. "At first I did not think I could endure. I was left with nothing but my own thoughts, and I felt utterly alone. Through contact with the Americans my father had become a Christian, and he then taught me and my family about God and Jesus. I began to pray every day and asked God for strength to live. He answered my prayers. I vowed to God that if I ever escaped the Khmer Rouge, I would serve Him and His children however He led me."

"Is that why you bring people here to the Church Health Center?" I asked.

"Yes, I know what it is like to be all alone and afraid. My people have all suffered terribly, and I think it is a small thing for me to take them to a doctor who will treat them with kindness. It is a way I can help ease the pain that we have all experienced in our home."

I am still very naive about Cambodian customs and ways of doing things. Fortunately, I have not repeated my mistake with Mrs. Nantawong, and I am always aware now that a person like Lelea is not working as a house-keeper in America just because it's a good job. Phen Phong has taught me about serving God in ways that I still do not completely understand. I still wonder whether I would have felt abandoned by God and would have cursed God rather than embraced Him as Phen Phong did. His example of faith is invigorating. Just seeing him makes me know that the human spirit can endure suffering that is almost too great to imagine and yet can still maintain the power to love and show compassion for others. Sometimes when I feel as though I am in a spiritual jungle, Phen Phong's example drives me to seek my own way out just as he did; and because of him, I know it can be done.

The Promise

Vera

The Church Health Center had been open less than three months when we found the Christmas of 1987 rapidly approaching. Thinking it would be fun to do so, I convinced Katherine, my nurse and future wife, to go Christmas caroling to a selected group of patients. Although reluctant at first, she finally agreed. So we made a list of our elderly patients we thought would enjoy a Christmastime visit. We also made a list of friends we hoped to entice into going with us.

On the Saturday before Christmas we set off as soon as it was dark to sing our way through Memphis. Our first two visits went well. Our patients were surprised but pleased that we had come. Everyone was having fun. Our third stop was to be at the home of Vera, a woman in her seventies whom I had seen several times for a variety of problems. In the office she was quite pleasant, and she was one of the first patients Katherine and I thought to put on our list.

We had trouble finding her street address. She lived on the edge of a rough part of town, and it was hard to see the street numbers in the dark. Finally we found what we thought was her apartment building. It was dark and somewhat foreboding, but our band of singers gallantly strode up the front steps and entered the building.

The halls were poorly lit, and we had to climb to the second floor.

"Katherine," I said, "are you sure this is the right place?"

"I think so," she said hesitantly.

We came to the apartment with the right number. I knocked on the door, and we prepared ourselves to be greeted warmly. Nothing happened. I knocked again. I could see through the transom that the light had been turned on, but no one came to the door. Everybody looked at me and began to suggest that we should go.

"Let me knock one more time," I said. "This is a really nice lady." I did not think it was too late to be calling. It was only seven o'clock in the evening. I banged loudly one more time. The door opened with the burglar chain still attached.

"What do you want?" a female voice barked gruffly.

"It's Doctor Morris and Katherine from the Church Health Center. We came to sing Christmas carols to you," I announced cheerfully.

"Go away. It's too late," the voice responded.

Not to be deterred, I begged, "Let us sing you a couple of songs before we leave."

"Oh, all right," she relented.

As quickly as possible we sang "O Come All Ye Faithful" and "Silent Night." Half the carolers were walking down the stairs before the last carol was done. I tried to wish Vera a merry Christmas through the door. As soon as I said the words, she said, "Good night," and shut the door firmly in my face.

In the car we tried to laugh about what had happened, but we felt so sad about it that we soon fell silent as we drove to the next house.

Our other experiences that night were much more pleasant, but I could not forget our encounter with Vera. Apparently, neither could she. When I saw her again in the office a couple of weeks later, she was full of apologies. "I was trying to give James a bath when you came, and I just couldn't stop to listen. I'm sorry because you were so nice to come and see me."

I had not realized until that moment that Vera did not live alone. She shared her apartment with James, who was also our patient.

James was only in his sixties, but he suffered the worst effects of a lifetime of alcohol abuse. His mind was similar to someone with Alzheimer's Disease, and his coordination was severely affected. He needed constant attention.

At first I thought James was Vera's husband or at least her boyfriend, but in time I realized that they lived together as a way of sharing expenses. It was a very good deal for James. With Vera he, in effect, got a live-in caregiver. She cooked for him, shopped for him, fed him, and even bathed him. That is quite a lot to expect from someone you live with only out of the necessity of sharing living expenses.

James had a son who brought him to the doctor, but it was Vera who looked out for him. I could tell it was an extraordinary burden on her and asked her, "Why do you continue to allow James to live with you?"

She looked at me, perplexed. "Where would he go? I just can't stand the thought of him going to a nursing home."

And so Vera and James continued to live the life of the "Odd Couple."

For a long time she and I laughed about our Christmas caroling fiasco. The more time passed, the more I was able to forget the oddity of it, and the more Vera could forget the embarrassment. Then one day I could tell that she had more on her mind than the aches and pains of her arthritis. She had a sheepish grin on her face, as though she were a child up to some kind of foolishness.

"Vera, what's going on that you're not telling me?" I asked.

"Doctor Morris," she looked up at me with her blue eyes. I realized I felt awkward having a person her age address me so formally, but she felt comfortable calling me Doctor. To do this probably gave her more confidence in my ability. "Doctor Morris, would you do me a big favor?"

I wondered what she could possibly be up to. "Of course, Vera, if I can."

"Well," she began slowly. "My nephew is getting married, and he's not exactly been a churchgoer and neither has his bride-to-be. But I told them about you, and they would really like for you to do the ceremony."

I was caught completely off guard. For a moment I was speechless. "When is it?" I asked.

"Next Saturday at my sister's house." She kept looking at me with those blue eyes.

"I'll be glad to, Vera, but I'll need to talk with them this week."

"I'll have Johnnie call you tomorrow," she promised.

Needless to say, Johnnie did not call me the next day. And when he called three days later, he did not really see the point of any kind of pre-marriage counseling. But I finally convinced him that we at least needed to meet to plan the wedding.

Our counseling session was brief, and we all agreed on a traditional service with traditional vows. The bride and groom fit the mold of many young, working-class people in Memphis who considered the church to be "full of hypocrites." Therefore they had abandoned any and all regular church involvement. I could not help hoping I might cause them to reconsider that conviction.

The day of the wedding I felt completely out of place. Almost everyone attending was from rural Mississippi, a culture with which I was totally unfamiliar. But they all received me as though they had known me all my life. They called me "Preacher," and I began to feel very comfortable with them. Before the ceremony, the women all gathered in the kitchen while the men stood on the front porch.

I stayed with the men until it was time for the service to begin. At that point I left the gathering on the porch and put on my robe in the back bedroom. When I came out, Vera was waiting for me. She had a tear in her eye.

"I'm so proud of you. I can't thank you enough for doing this for my family. We may not have much, but we've got each other." I reached out and hugged her; then I walked into the living room and called the men and women to come together.

I took my place in front of the television set while the
bride and groom stood before me. It was a brief service,
but as pleasant as any wedding I have been a part of. When
it was over, people came up to me and said what is always
said to the minister: "That was the most beautiful service
I've ever seen."

I recall that while the service was in progress, I felt a
bond with this family, and it seemed like I belonged; but as
soon as the last *amen* was said, I again felt a stranger and
an outsider. Despite several pleas for me to stay for the
reception, I excused myself, made my way to my car, and
drove home.

Along the way I realized that my dual role of physician
and minister had just given me an experience I would
otherwise never have had. I had once again been asked to
share an intimacy with people that only my professional
credentials allowed to happen.

It never occurred to me that this experience with Vera's
family was to be only the beginning of getting to know
them extremely well. Soon after the wedding a variety of
family members became my patients. Phyllis, Luther,
Leroy, and Martha each came with his or her own unique
problems and concerns. In time, one developed lung cancer and died; one had ovarian cancer and also died. During
this time I learned many of the family dynamics—some
good, many not so good.

This process was just beginning when I had my second
experience with the gathered family. This time Vera called
the center and left a message that only I could help her
with her problem. When I called her back, I could tell she
felt a sense of urgency. "I just didn't know who else to

call," she began. "Everyone in the family agreed that you are like a member of the family now, and you were the one to do it."

"Do what, Vera?"

"Oh, I'm sorry. I hate to ask you again, but my niece Velma's boy has died, and they are bringing him back here to bury him. I wouldn't ask you, but everyone thought you would do such a nice job."

I tried to get out of performing the funeral service but to no avail. "Vera, isn't there a minister of a church he grew up in who knew him and who would be better to do the service?"

"He's lived out there in San Francisco for so long and has been gone for such a long time, there's no one here who knows him," she responded.

I surmised that he had died of AIDS and was gay, but no one was ever to say either of those words. So I agreed to do the funeral of a man I had never met and who, it seemed, was really known by very few of his family members. It was a difficult task, but Vera's insistence was hard to resist.

Many of the people I had met at the wedding were also at the funeral. The bride and groom paid me their respects, and several people told me again how wonderful the wedding had been. Some of my new patients tried to call me aside for a quick consultation about a new ache or pain.

I was moved by how many people came to the funeral of a man who had left Mississippi so many years before. Few of them had more than vague memories of him, but still they came. It was, for me, a sign of how powerful the

family can be and how the experience of the death of a
young man can affect even those only remotely touched by
it. It was Vera, though, who seemed to have a true sadness
about his death. She remembered him when he was a child.
"He was the sweetest little boy," she said with tears in
her eyes. Again I felt a little strange being there. I thought
that for some of these people I might be becoming a sort
of rent-a-preacher for the family. I was not interested in
doing that, but I felt a bond with Vera that I wanted to
act on. I realized I was glad she wanted me to perform the
service.

For the past ten years Vera has come to the Church
Health Center every two or three months. Sometimes she
sees me and sometimes she sees Dr. White or Dr. Wallace.
Whenever I see her, I feel her smiling at me, and I can sense
the warmth and depth of emotion she has for me.

Two years ago, she again told me she had a favor to ask
of me. I quickly began to think of excuses as to why I
couldn't do whatever she was about to ask for.

"Doctor Morris, I want you to promise me that when I
die, you'll be there to do my funeral. Will you do that?"
She looked up at me and smiled.

I nodded. "I hope it's not for a long time, but if I'm still
around, Vera, I'll be there with you if that's what you
want."

She sighed with relief, "I've been trying to get my
courage up to ask you, and now I feel so much better."

Her request has only sealed the bond between us.
Every six months or so she catches my eye when I pass
her in the hall and she asks, "Do you remember your
promise?"

I laugh and say, "I haven't forgotten." And I can see her smile.

Neither I nor the Church Health Center has done anything particularly special for Vera over the years. We have given her routine care in a manner that she can afford, and on two occasions I have used my ministerial office to perform the ordinances of life for her and members of her family. In the overall scope of things, those gestures are quite small, but it doesn't feel that way to me and I suspect it doesn't to Vera.

I have come to think that the things that matter most in life may be those small aspects of living—those ceremonies and rituals that mark events of life. Frequently, such experiences have much more meaning and impact than the seemingly monumental experiences we expect to be profoundly transforming.

Every four to eight weeks Vera makes a financial contribution to the Health Center. She sends $20 to $40 as regularly as clockwork. These gifts matter just as much as a $10,000 check. Vera gives her gifts out of a full knowledge of what the Health Center is all about because of her years of experience in dealing with it. She sends money she can ill afford to give up, but she does so cheerfully and repeatedly because she knows it is valued, just as she is valued when she comes as a patient. What I don't think she fully understands is the impact her faithfulness and trust in us has on us. While I know that no one on our staff can live up to the exalted view that she may hold about us, I know we must be doing something right. Vera knows that she is loved, not necessarily by anyone in particular, but by our community which exists to demonstrate the love of

God at work in the world. And her certainty and faith in us and our ministry speak volumes to us as individuals and as a group. Those things that each of us has done for Vera seem small, almost inconsequential, but taken together I believe they are powerful. And that is what this work is all about and what will ultimately make the work enduring. The collective actions of the staff at the Center are greater than the sum of the actions of the individuals because of God's action in and through us.

Checking Out of Life

Phillip

One bright, fall morning, I walked across the street to enter the health center after coming back from a meeting downtown. As I walked toward the front door, a man in his early forties opened it for me and let me in. His hair had a touch of gray and was short-cropped. He was a little overweight and about my height, so that I looked him in the eye as I passed him at the door. He was polite and kind and seemed somewhat melancholy.

I thanked him for opening the door, then ran up the stairs to get my white coat and started to work. I was a few minutes late getting back from the meeting, which was always the case, and the exam rooms were already filled with patients waiting to see me. I started right in trying to catch up as soon as I could.

After seeing six or seven patients, I quickly recognized the patient in the next room as the man at the door. His name was Phillip, and he had come about his high blood pressure. He was new to Memphis and had run out of his medicine. He was so well spoken and obviously well educated, I was having trouble understanding why he was in the position of needing to seek care from us.

"Phillip," I asked; "what brings you to Memphis?"

"I'd never been here, so I thought I'd give it a try," he said.

This was an odd answer, so I kept on pushing. "So where are you staying?"

"Here and there," he said.

Once again, the answer for someone who is homeless.

"Where will you stay tonight?" I asked.

"Oh, I'll find someplace. I always do," he quickly responded.

"Phillip, how did you end up homeless?" I was intrigued.

"Oh, it's a long story. You don't have time to hear it all," he said, with his head bowed.

"I've got time," I said, even though I knew that the waiting room was filled with people.

Phillip then began to tell me a long story—gut-wrenching at every turn. Ten years earlier on Christmas Eve, he and his family had gone to a church service at the local United Methodist Church. At the time, he was teaching high school science in Indiana. He had two master's degrees, one in biology and one in education. Teaching in the public schools seemed perfect for him. He liked the challenge of working with teenagers and looked forward to when his own daughters would be older and growing up. At the time, they were five, seven, and nine, perfectly spaced and still at ages where they worshiped their daddy. But as much fun as it was while they were young, he looked forward to the day he could share "ideas" with them. His wife spent her days looking after the kids and the home. She always prepared dinner for him and tried to make their house the perfect Midwestern home.

That Christmas Eve he was singing in the church choir and drove himself to the church early. His wife and children came later. He remembered the service as full of singing and reverence.

"It was what Christmas Eve should be like," he said. When the service was over, the family walked out of church together and headed home. The girls all rode with their mother, and he led the way in his car. A thousand times over he has relived what happened next.

"As I was pulling out of the church parking lot, I turned right onto the highway. There was plenty of room for my wife to come right behind me, but for some reason she hesitated. I was watching her car in my rearview mirror. I guess she thought I was going to get too far ahead of her. I don't know, but all of a sudden she pulled out onto the highway right in front of an oncoming truck. I couldn't believe what I was seeing in the mirror. It was like watching a movie. Her car turned over and over and then before I knew it, it exploded.

"At first I did not believe what I was seeing; then I threw open the door and ran back toward them. By the time I got there, they were already gone. The fire was so hot I could not get close to the car, but I knew right away they were all dead. They were all dead. They were all dead."

He fell silent.

I didn't know what to say. Phillip kept looking at me with tears running down his face. Finally I said, "I'm so sorry, Phillip. I can't imagine anything so awful. What did you do next?"

"There was nothing I could do. I felt completely numb, and I still do. I guess you could say I checked out of life. I couldn't go back to teaching. I had nothing to live for. So I just walked out of town and started wandering the country. I've been in all 48 states and crossed the country ten times in the last ten years. I'm tired of roaming, but I don't know what else to do. It all seems so long ago, but it feels like yesterday."

I could think of nothing I could do to help him. Giving him his blood pressure medicine was not going to solve his problem. I had only one idea.

"Phillip, there is a shelter just down the street that you might want to try and stay at. It's called Genesis House. Would you like for me to call now?"

"Sure, maybe it's time for me to stop running."

With those words, I began to wonder if we could really help Phillip get his life back. I was committed to doing whatever I could. The director of Genesis House readily agreed to give Phillip a room. I made a plan to see Phillip back at the center in a week, ostensibly to check his blood pressure but really to see what else I might do to help him back into the world of the living.

When Phillip came back, he seemed to be in a cheerful mood.

"How is it going?" I asked.

"It's going real well. I like it there," he said with a smile.

I was encouraged. Maybe he was ready to start over.

During the next several months I saw him frequently. Every time was more encouraging than the last. He began talking about settling down in Memphis. He thought maybe he could get a job teaching again, but mostly he could just stop running. Every time I saw him he would talk to me about his philosophy of life—about things he had learned from living on the streets for the last ten years. I hung on his every word. It was not that what he had to say was profound, but it came out of a depth of experience that I could only imagine.

Then one day he asked me a question. "They tell me you are also a minister, is that true?"

"Yes, Phillip, it is."

"Well, do you think your church would be willing to have someone like me come to it?" It was a question that had only one answer.

"We would love to have you, Phillip."

The next Sunday he came to St. John's and sat on the back pew. From my seat up front I could see him. At first, he stayed to himself, but later he began talking to the other people who sat in the back. I could tell he was getting more comfortable.

Then he surprised me when, at the end of a Sunday morning service, he walked down the aisle during the singing of the last hymn and asked to join the church. I was pleased he wanted to be a member, but I was leery about whether he was ready to be a part of a congregation again. He seemed extremely happy as people welcomed him to the congregation at the end of the service.

Three weeks later I saw him in the clinic. After discussing his medical problems, he asked, "Do you think they would let me sing in the choir? You know, I used to sing in the choir in Indiana, and I still like to do it. I've noticed the church's choir could use a few more bodies."

I smiled because he obviously knew that a small church like ours is always desperate for people willing to sing in the choir.

"I think they would be happy to have you. Why don't you ask the choir director?"

The next Sunday, Phillip walked down the aisle just ahead of me as the choir processed in front of the ministers. Several times during the service I looked over at him, and I could tell he was enjoying himself. Every Sunday for the next several weeks it was the same.

The next time I saw him in the office, however, things had changed. I could tell he was anxious about something.

"What's the problem?" I asked.

"Genesis House has told me that I need to find a job soon or I can't stay there anymore. I'm not sure I'm ready for that." He was obviously upset.

"Well, Phillip, don't you think it might be time to give it a try? You don't have to teach. It can be something simple, just to prove you can do it." He thought for a minute, then seemed to have a change of heart.

"I guess you're right. I've got to start somewhere."

The next week he began working part time at a local grocery store as a sacker. I would see him walk to work early in the morning as I was driving to the health center. I would wave, and he would wave back with a big smile. Every Sunday after church he would grab me and tell me how it was going.

"I really think I can make it this time. I'm saving up my money for my own apartment and should have enough to move out on my own in about six weeks." He seemed excited, and I was happy for him.

As the six weeks passed, every week I could tell he was becoming a little more anxious about the impending move. One Sunday he was filled with doubts.

"I'm not sure I'm ready for this." He was trembling.

"You are ready, Phillip. You've been getting to this point for months, and I know you can do it." I tried to be encouraging.

"Do you really think I can?" He was like a small child. I patted him on the back. "I'm sure you can."

The week before he was to move, he seemed all excited about what was about to happen.

"I really think I'm ready," he told me. I wished him well and held my breath.

He was not at church the next Sunday. I asked David, the choir director, if he knew where he was, and he said he had not heard a thing. I thought that Phillip might have had to work at the grocery store, or perhaps he was enjoying his new apartment so much he decided to sleep in. There are a hundred reasons why people miss church, and I was sure he had at least one of them.

The next day he also missed his doctor's appointment. That had never happened. I was still hopeful that there was a good reason, but I was starting to feel uneasy. I called the director of Genesis House.

"Do you know what has happened to Phillip?" I asked. There was silence on the other end.

"I guess I should have called you," he said.

"What happened?" I waited to hear.

"When the day came for him to move out, he was in a panic. He came to me and said, 'I can't do this. I can't believe you are making me leave. You're just like all the rest. I'm getting out of here.' He went to his room, packed his bags and walked out the front door. Nobody has seen him since."

I thanked him for telling me the story and hung up. I felt sick to my stomach. What had gone wrong? Had I pushed him too far? Should we have done more to prepare him for the move? I had a thousand questions and no answers. He was just gone.

I have never learned what happened to Phillip. For several years his picture as a new member of St. John's hung in the vestibule of the sanctuary, and I would look at it every Sunday. For a long time I held onto the unrealistic hope that he might come back or at least write a letter. That has never happened. I have often wondered why his life took the course it did in the first place. Many people have lost their families through tragedies and not "checked out of life" the way Phillip did. Maybe his story was not even true, but I believe it was.

How many homeless men and women have stories similar to Phillip's? How much tragedy fills the shelters of America every night? I suspect if we really knew, it could break even the hardest heart.

I have never really understood what happened between Phillip and me during the six months that I knew him. He gave me a wake-up call about the limits of what we could do to help people to change. But I like to believe that the experience of kindness and love he felt while he was in Memphis must have affected him in a way he could not soon forget.

Is he still wandering the country aimlessly? Did he return to Indiana? Is he dead? Who's to say? Since my experience with Phillip, I have never looked the same way at someone who is homeless. I am always aware that whatever the outside veneer may look like, there is always a heart inside which is aching.

I have also never seen Christmas in the same way since then. For many people Christmas brings only sadness and not joy. But I continue to hope that the joy that inspires the Christmas spirit, God's love and compassion, can in time touch even a heart as grief-stricken as Phillip's.

The New Coat

Matthew

My office at the Church Health Center is on the second floor of our original building. It is in what used to be one of the bedrooms when the house was used as a home. My desk is situated so that I can look out the large double-hung window that faces the street. I placed my desk so I can look at the church across the street and see the huge oak tree at the entrance to the courtyard which leads to the door of the church.

Before I moved to Memphis, the church placed a wooden bench under the tree at the street's edge; the bench is used by those waiting for the bus which stops at the corner of Peabody and Bellevue.

Over the years, at various times of the day, I have been able to look out the window and see people sitting on the bench waiting for the bus. Then one day a number of years ago, I do not remember just when, I began seeing Matthew sitting on the bench for most of the day, virtually every day.

At first I thought he must be a homeless man; he sort of had the look. He's a big man—tall, with big bones. He was obviously strong at one time because you can see muscles in his arms that suggest he was once powerful. His clothes are worn. He often sports a hat, and he almost always wears suspenders.

In our neighborhood, it is not unusual to see transient men who are very visible for a week or two and who then move on. Seeing Matthew sitting on the bench, I assumed at first that this was the case with him, until one day I saw him stand and begin to walk down the street. He has the obvious movements of someone who has had a stroke, even though he is only in his early fifties. He walks with his left arm straight and slightly bent at the elbow, and he swings his left leg out to the side before he pulls it forward to take a step. His gait is slow and slightly unsteady, and he walks with a cane in his right hand. When I first saw him walk, I began to wonder what his story really was, and I hoped he was not having to sleep on the street.

In the beginning I did not know his name but would nod hello to him whenever I walked across the street to go to the church. He would always smile, raise his good hand, and say, "Hello."

One day as I was passing, I stopped briefly and said, "You know if you ever need to see the doctor, you can make an appointment at that place across the street."

He looked at me and smiled, then said, "Thank you," and went back to his thoughts while sitting on the bench.

About two weeks later, as I entered an exam room to meet a new patient, I recognized the man who was becoming a familiar fixture on the bench. It was then that I learned his name is Matthew.

Matthew was in his early fifties when he had a stroke. Apparently he was a victim of severe uncontrolled hypertension. He had worked for twenty years as a janitor in a factory when he awoke one morning and could not move the left side of his body. His thinking was also somewhat impaired. I had a hard time learning the details of Matthew's life. He seemed always quick to say, "Yes, sir," or, "No, sir," but he was not able to form a lot of sentences to tell his story.

Before the stroke, he had made enough money to pay his bills and have his own apartment. But afterwards, he had to struggle to make ends meet. I don't know who, but someone, a social worker I suspect, helped him get on disability and find a rooming house that he could afford. It so happened that his room was located just down the street from the health center and the church; and for whatever reason, Matthew found his bench and began to make our corner his home.

When I first saw Matthew, despite his stroke he was still not on any blood pressure medicine, and his blood pressure was quite high. I asked him, "Why aren't you taking any medicine?" He stopped smiling and looked at the floor.

"Is the problem that you can't afford it?"

He nodded his head yes.

"You don't need to worry, Matthew, we can give you your medicine here."

At that point, Matthew looked up from the floor and, looking at me, said, "Thank you."

From that point on I felt a bond with Matthew. I felt certain that Matthew was glad to have someone watching out for him. I think that was partly why he became a fixture on the bus bench.

From then on, at every visit, I not only worried about Matthew's blood pressure, but also other aspects of his life. Our pastoral counselor made sure his disability check was coming to him and not being taken by someone else, as is often the case for people in Matthew's situation. Fortunately, everything was okay.

Soon Matthew began showing up regularly for the church's soup kitchen, which is open three days a week. To make sure he was not coming because he didn't have any food, I asked him, "Why do you come to the soup kitchen?"

He answered simply, "I just like being here."

He obviously felt some sense of fellowship, and he began to take on little roles of responsibility. Often, after the meal was served, Matthew would help to pick up any trash that was thrown on the grounds outside the church doors. He would also help set up and take down chairs in the dining hall even though he had only one good arm. It was awkward for him to do it, but he seemed to get satisfaction out of it. A little later, I began to see him help the church custodian sweep the sidewalk on Sunday morning and take out the trash before church members arrived. He was making himself a member of the church staff, if not an active member of the church.

When I saw him as a patient, I tried to think of ways to make his life easier. He walked with a four-pronged cane that had long since lost its rubber handle and feet. The four prongs at the end of the cane helped him keep his balance, but without the rubber tips, he was prone to slip.

To replace the rubber handle, he used an old rag to form a cushion to hold onto so the metal did not rub his hand. We are often given such canes by families when an elderly loved one dies, and I gave him a new cane during one of his visits. I handed it to him proudly saying, "Matthew, I think this cane will work a lot better than the one you have."

He smiled and quietly said, "Thank you."

He took it in his right hand and walked out with it while hanging the old one on the crook of his arm. I was proud to give him something he clearly needed. Yet two days later I noticed he was back using the old cane and today, several years later, he is still using a rag around the handle for the same cane. Perhaps there is something about its familiarity that is comforting to him.

After a while, Matthew became known by members of my staff and by the church. Having him around became familiar. If he was not present on a Sunday morning, members of my Sunday School would ask about him. He was always friendly and waved to me as I came and went.

One Sunday morning after church, however, Matthew appeared to be anxious in a way I had never seen before. After church, I started to cross the street to go to my office for a few minutes. I walked past Matthew's bench and turned to tell him good-bye only to find him nervously standing in front of the bench looking down the street. It was a cold, January day. I walked on across the street, entered the health center, and walked up the stairs to my office.

Once in the warm building, I remembered Matthew and looked out of my office to see what he was up to. He was still looking nervously down the street. I watched for a moment until a car drove up and stopped in front of him. Out of the car stepped Joy and Scott Sutherland, members of my Sunday School class. Until that moment, I did not realize that Joy and Scott had any special fondness for Matthew, but what I then observed made me know that was not the case.

As Matthew stood by the road, Joy walked over to him and helped him take off his coat. It was a thin, cloth coat, probably okay for cool spring nights but not adequate for a cold January day.

As Joy helped him take off the coat, Scott opened the trunk of the car and took out a heavy, beige overcoat with a thick, brown lining. Like Matthew, Scott is a big man. It was obviously an old coat of Scott's, but it fit Matthew just fine. Joy buttoned the coat for him and made sure that it was the right size. It was.

I could read Matthew's lips. "Thank you," was all he said. Then he smiled.

Joy and Scott had a few more words to say, and then they got in their car and drove away. Matthew watched them until they were out of sight and then he calmly sat down on the bench and became lost in his thoughts.

I sat back down at my desk and thought about what I had seen—a young couple, unaware that I was watching, performed an act of kindness for someone who could only respond by saying, "Thank you." There would be no reciprocal act. They could expect nothing in return. Joy's gentleness and Scott's kindness defined for me what acts of discipleship and servant ministry are supposed to be.

For the next few weeks, while it remained cold, Matthew could be seen on his bench every day just as usual. Unlike his return to his old cane, however, Matthew continued to wear his new coat.

In 1995 I lost Matthew as a patient for a while when the state of Tennessee began its Medicaid managed care program known as TennCare. Because of his disability, Matthew qualified for Medicaid and could go to any doctor who would accept it. Although our main mission at the Church Health Center is to care for the working poor who are uninsured, we will often make exceptions for people like Matthew. When TennCare began, however, patients with Medicaid were assigned to managed care organizations which operated like an HMO. Each company has its own pool of doctors, and patients are assigned to a specific doctor who acts as a gatekeeper.

When TennCare began, there was a mad scramble by companies to enroll patients who could choose the MCO of their preference even though most patients had no idea what the consequences of their choice might be. A couple of companies went so far as to offer people turkeys or credit cards for signing up with their company.

If a person did not pick an MCO, he or she was randomly assigned to a company and then randomly assigned to a doctor. Such was the case with Matthew. I am sure he did not understand the instructions that were sent to him, and there was no one to help him make a wise choice.

After six months went by without seeing him in the office, I asked him if he had forgotten his appointment.

"Matthew," I asked, "do we need to make you a new appointment to see me?"

"No," he answered. "They said I can't see you anymore."

"Who is 'they'?" I asked.

"The people who gave me this card."

I looked at the card he handed me. He was assigned to an MCO which we did not work with, and his doctor's office was in Germantown, a suburb of Memphis that might as well be in New York for the likelihood of Matthew finding his way to his new doctor's office. I shook my head in frustration and took him across the street and asked Kim to try and straighten things out for him.

It took calling every day for almost a week for Kim to get permission for Matthew to return to my care, but finally he was allowed once again to be treated by me. This was an exasperating experience which has been repeated many times since Tennessee has instituted managed care for the Medicaid-eligible population. Matthew's experience reflects what can happen when reforms undertaken for primarily financial reasons masquerade as programs to help the poor. The indigent person, like Matthew, often ends up worse off than when he started.

Fortunately for Matthew, since the misadventure with TennCare, his life has been fairly stable. He has a routine, which he follows most days. He begins each day by helping the church custodian clean up in one fashion or other. He then sits on his bench for most of the day and also takes long walks, meandering around our building and around the church. In the afternoon he is again helping where he can to keep the church clean. On days when the soup kitchen is open, he is first in line and last to leave. At the end of the day he returns to his room down the street.

So it went for Matthew, until one Sunday morning there was a slight change in his normal routine. As the 11 o'clock church service began, I was in my usual place at the front of the sanctuary making the announcements about the events for the week. As I was welcoming visitors, I could not help seeing Matthew being led to a pew by a member of the congregation, George Wilson. George, a retired writer, had decided, on his own, that it was past time for Matthew to be left sitting on the bench outside while the worship service went on inside. Why had it taken so long for someone to invite Matthew to be a part of the congregation? Why had I not done the same thing as George?

Throughout the service I could not help looking time and again at George and Matthew sitting and standing together. When a hymn was sung, George helped Matthew find his place. During the sermon, Matthew seemed to be paying as much attention as anyone else. It was wonderful to see him there. At least on that day, I felt that our congregation truly did reflect the body of Christ in all its brokenness and its glory.

Since that day, Matthew has come to the worship service or to the Fellowship Hall from time to time. He is still shy about coming on his own, but I believe he knows he is welcome. On the day I looked out of my office window and saw Matthew's coat, I was moved to witness an act of kindness which sought no reward. For me, Matthew's presence is a daily reminder of the broken nature of our world and the need to always be ready to care for a brother such as Matthew and to reach out for his hand every day.

But it is not enough to just feed him, clothe him, or care for him when he is sick. We must also sit with him and worship beside him because he is an equal in the family of

God. I can't say that I do this every day because I know I don't; but thanks to Matthew's perseverance and daily presence, I have done it more than I would have before he came to us, and that's a start.

"I Think You Have a Problem"

Arthur

"Well, Katherine, what did you think of him?" I asked after she finished interviewing the medical assistant that the Medical Society employment service sent us.

"I think he'll be okay," she said. "He'll fit in fine since his last name is Church." And so, we hired our first medical assistant, whose job it would be to support and to help keep the volunteer doctor and nurse happy on the night shift and on Saturdays.

In the beginning of the Church Health Center, Katherine and I figured we would do fine in the daytime having one doctor and one nurse to take care of any problems we would face. But because we would have different volunteer doctors and nurses each night, we needed a staff person who knew where everything was kept and who could give a sense of continuity. This person could also keep us informed about what happened at night and tell us which patients we needed to follow up on.

Neither of us had worked with a medical assistant before, and we didn't know what to expect. What sort of skills did he have? How far could we trust his judgment? Arthur was in his mid-twenties but had already worked for several years as a medical assistant in Detroit. He and his mother had recently moved to Memphis, and this was going to be his first job here.

He was extremely pleasant, friendly, and eager to please. From the first, the volunteers liked him. After working with him only one time, the volunteer doctor or nurse would later tell Katherine and me, "You can go home now. Arthur will take care of me." It was reassuring for us to hear that they had confidence in him, and it was wonderful for us to be able to go home before nine o'clock at night.

Arthur would come to work at noon and work beside Katherine in the afternoon. This allowed her to teach him her method of nursing and also assess his skills and weaknesses. We quickly learned that Arthur sometimes had more confidence than was warranted. For example, he was eager to let me know that he had experience in casting fractures, even though I myself was sometimes unsure about how to apply a cast for a certain broken bone. Katherine took him in tow. She was able to direct his enthusiasm into other projects, and he seemed to understand the role we were defining for him.

During the first six months that the Church Health Center was open, Arthur worked extremely well with us as part of the team. He seemed to understand what we were about and helped to create the attitude we wanted to convey both to patients and to volunteers. Sometimes, however, he was a little too proud, and he exaggerated to people on the phone, "This is Arthur *Church* of the *Church* Health Center." Katherine would give him the evil eye whenever she overheard him talking that way, and, in time, he switched to just referring to himself as Arthur.

One evening Arthur said to me, "Doc, do you mind looking at this problem I've got? It's starting to bother me a little."

"Certainly, Arthur, what can I do for you?" I had no idea to what he was referring.

"Well," he said, "it's a little embarrassing. Can we go into one of the exam rooms?"

"Sure," I said, and we walked down to Room 3, the smallest of our rooms. "What's the problem?" I sat down on the doctor's stool.

"I've got this swelling in my testicle," he said.

I began thinking that he might have a hernia, but there was only one way to tell.

"Pull your pants down, Arthur, and let's take a look." I turned my back to him as he got undressed, and I put on the examination gloves. When I turned around, it was all I could do to keep my mouth from falling open.

Arthur's right testicle was the size of a grapefruit.

My first thought was to wonder how he could walk without it causing him pain or getting in the way. I tried to stay calm and asked him, "How long has it been this way?"

He, too, tried to stay calm and replied matter-of-factly, "It's been getting big for about six months."

I shook my head and muttered, "Uh, huh."

I then sat down on the stool and reached to feel his testicle. At this point I was almost to the point of divorcing myself from the awareness that this was Arthur, my medical assistant whom I had grown to like, and was almost able to regard him as a patient that I was meeting for the first time. However, it was all I could do to remain objective. Arthur's testicle was rock-hard. His scrotum was not filled with fluid. This was not a hernia. It was not a cyst. There was little doubt in my mind that he had testicular cancer. What to do next?

I finished the exam and then asked Arthur to pull his pants up. I removed my gloves and began to wash my hands while my mind was racing, trying to think of what to tell him.

"Arthur," I said as gently as I knew how, "I think you have a problem." What could be more obvious, I thought to myself. "There are several things this could be, but one of them is cancer. I'm not sure about it, but we need to find out."

"Yeah, I sort of thought that myself," he said, again very matter-of-factly. I could not tell whether he really thought that and knew the consequences, or if this was another case of his appearing too sure of himself.

"I'll make sure we get an answer as soon as possible and get it taken care of right away."

"Thanks, Doc."

We walked out of the room together, and I immediately scheduled the appropriate test for the next day, making an appointment for Arthur to see Dr. Shelton, a young urologist I had grown to respect.

When I told Katherine the problem, she too was speechless. How could we have been working beside him all this time and not have known anything about what was going on?

Within 48 hours Arthur's tumor was removed. Fortunately, it was the type of testicular cancer that responds well to treatment. He would be sore for a few weeks, but he had reason to believe that he would be cured.

After only a couple of weeks, Arthur was back at work. He seemed like his old self. He resumed his duties as though nothing had happened. Soon, however, Katherine and I both noticed that Arthur seemed very moody at times. He would make a mistake, Katherine would correct him, and he would then pout for the rest of the day like a young child. She and I both wrote it off as the effects of dealing with the cancer. Anyone could understand his change in mood.

During the next six months, Arthur missed work sometimes and would call in sick at the last minute. On one occasion, he called to say he was in Nashville, had a flat tire, and would not be at work that day. His explanation didn't make sense; and, despite his cancer, his excuses were beginning to get irritating.

Over the next several months, the problem got worse. His absences were more frequent, and his attitude was often hostile. There was something wrong, but what? Was he depressed about his cancer? Was he having trouble facing his own mortality? I was sympathetic to his problem, but I needed him to do his job better. I needed to be able to depend on him.

Then one Monday, Arthur did not show up for work, and he didn't call. I called his home and talked to his mother. She didn't know where he was. The next day he didn't call, and he didn't come to work. The same thing happened on Wednesday and Thursday. I was worried. His mother was frantic, and everyone in the office was upset, wondering what had happened to him. On Thursday night the local evening news led with a story that made my heart sink. The unidentified body of a young African-American man had been found in the back of a U-Haul truck in North Memphis. He had apparently been dead for four to five days. I was sure it was Arthur.

When he did not call on Friday, I was even more convinced that the body was his. All I knew to do was wait and pray that he would turn up alive.

Over the weekend, the body was identified. It was not Arthur. On Monday I told Kim that if Arthur were to call, I wanted to talk to him before anyone else. That afternoon, he walked into the office and asked to speak to me.

When I saw him, I was at first thankful that he was alive, but I quickly felt my feelings of relief turn to anger. There was little he could say that would make me want to let him keep his job.

We walked upstairs to my office and sat down. He sat in an overstuffed green chair, and I sat across from him. He hung his head and held his hands in his lap.

"Well," I began. "Where have you been?"

"I've been holed up in a hotel smoking crack for the last week."

"That's what you've been doing while we have all been worried whether you were dead or alive?" I shot back.

In a soft voice, he said, "Yeah, that's what I've been doing—day and night, 24 hours a day. I've been smoking crack. After the first day, I thought I could quit and come to work and say I was sick, but I didn't want to quit. I just kept smoking. After the second day, I said, 'What the hell' and just kept on. By Friday, I couldn't think straight and hated myself for what I'd done. And that's pretty much where I am now." He then fell silent.

What was I to do? I knew that people were inclined to smoke crack for long periods of time, but five days straight without a break? I couldn't believe it, but I somehow knew that this time he was telling me the truth. "What do you expect me to do, Arthur? Tell you to go downstairs, put on your lab coat and get back to work?"

"No, I didn't know what you'd do, but I needed to face the music." He seemed a little more animated, but I could tell the pain he felt was real.

My mind was reeling as to what I should do. On one hand, I wanted to reach out and help him, but I was so angry at what he had done and how callously he had treated his friends and co-workers.

"So, Arthur, if you want, I will try and get you in a drug treatment program, but you can't keep working here."

"That's what I thought you'd say." He paused. "I need help to deal with this problem." There were tears in his eyes. I wanted to reach out and hold him, but the anger held me back.

All I could do was pat him on the back and say, "I've got a friend who runs a drug treatment program. I'll go give him a call." And so I left and set in motion the process for Arthur to be admitted for his crack cocaine addition.

For the next twenty-eight days he began to deal with this demon which was crushing the life out of him. Several nights after I left the center I went to visit him to see how he was doing. Kim, the receptionist, reached out to him much further and went with his mother to AlAnon meetings, which help the family members of people with substance abuse problems. She also listened to his pain as he wrestled with the dark side of his soul.

When Arthur finished his in-patient stay, I was not inclined to keep in touch with him. I felt wounded by what he had done. My trust was violated, and I could not see letting him back into the "family" of the Church Health Center. I had done all I could do. I wished him well, but he was no longer a part of my everyday life.

During the next two years I thought about Arthur from time to time but made no effort to contact him. After a while, I no longer felt angry, but neither was I inclined to rebuild a relationship with him. He became part of my past, and I could not imagine that he would ever be part of my present again. Then one day, for reasons that have no explanation, I reached for the phone and called to see how he was doing. His mother answered the phone.

"Mrs. Church, this is Doctor Morris at the Church Health Center. I am calling to talk to Arthur."

"Arthur," she said almost matter-of-factly, "is in the hospital."

"He is?" I was startled. "What for?"

"The cancer came back. He's getting treatment."

I was shocked. That's not supposed to happen. He should have been cured long ago. "Where is he?" I asked.

"The Med," she said and gave me his room number.

I knew right away if he was in the Med, he did not have health insurance and was no longer seeing Dr. Shelton. That afternoon I made the time to go see him. I was not sure what I would say, and I didn't know what to expect.

When I found his room, he was in a bed in one of the last of the wards of the city hospital. There were six people in the same room, and his bed was in the corner with the curtains partially drawn around it. But I could see him when I walked into the room. He immediately recognized me and scrambled to get out of bed. Only to do so he had to reach for a cane. He needed it to stand. He took a couple of halting steps toward me before I stopped him. He was thin—he looked like someone with cancer—but he seemed glad to see me.

"So how come you're here?" was how I began the conversation.

"Well, I began having pain in my leg, and I just thought I had pulled something until all of a sudden, I had this sharp pain and couldn't walk. It turns out the cancer had spread to the big bone in my leg and it just suddenly broke. That's why I'm having a little trouble getting around."

I tried to smile, but I felt sick to my stomach. Whenever someone has a pathologic fracture from metastasis of a cancer, it is never good news. Often it signals the approach of death. Was Arthur about to die? At this point, I forgot the problems surrounding his drug abuse and only remembered how it was when he first came to work for us. My heart ached for him, but I knew there was nothing I could do to help him.

"They tell me that they have a good treatment for this, but it will take a while for my leg to heal." He was able to smile while he told me the treatment plan. I listened intently but doubted whether his progress was as good as he was being led to believe.

He then told me how he had been working as a janitor at the Mid-South Coliseum when his leg broke. It was clear his life had been hard since I last saw him, but he was quick to tell me, "I've been off the drugs for almost two years." I was happy to hear that.

After 15 minutes, I ran out of things to talk about. We did not have a lot in common, and I did not know how to make small talk with him. I wished him well, left the hospital, and returned to work. For the next several days I could not get him out of my mind, but I did not know what to do for him. I did nothing.

To my amazement, Arthur responded dramatically to the cancer treatment. Slowly his leg healed, and within six months there was no sign of the tumor. Because he had to go to the doctor several times a week and often felt sick immediately after the treatment, he was unable to work. In order to pass his days, Arthur began to learn how to play golf. He became an avid player. Golf became his great love.

I was extremely happy that Arthur had recovered from his ordeal; but once he did, I lost touch with him for the next two years. During this time, the health center grew, and once again we had need of a medical assistant. After pondering about where we should turn to find the right person, Katherine and I discussed the possibility of offering the job to Arthur. It would be a risk. Even if his prior problems were behind him, he had not worked as a medical assistant in years. He would, in effect, be starting over. Katherine was willing to give him a chance, so I called him and asked if he would come and talk to me about a job.

"Arthur," I said, "would you consider coming back to work for us in your old job?" I could tell he was stunned.

"Do you really want me back?" he said.

"I wouldn't be talking if we didn't think you could do it." I could tell he was pleased, and I knew instantly he would accept our offer.

He agreed that we could test him for drugs without any warning at any time. He began almost immediately. I could tell he was happy to be back, but at first he had a hard time adjusting. During the time he had been gone, our staff had grown tremendously. There were now four doctors and five nurses. Now, he was the third medical assistant. There was a lot for him to learn. At first he was defensive and would make excuses for mistakes he made. But that did not last very long.

Within a few months, he was back working at night taking care of the volunteers. Some of the long-time volunteers were extremely happy to see him again. And it did not take long for the newer volunteers to say to me, "You can go home now. Arthur will take care of me."

On an almost daily basis, I see people in situations that seem nearly hopeless, either because the disease they are facing appears to be fatal or because their living situation or their behavior has devastated their lives to the point that life seems irreparable. On two occasions Arthur faced the worst that life has to offer, and he not only survived but overcame an awful way of living. I am sure that he, like all of us, struggles daily with the hardships of life, but he has faced the worst of times and has come through them with the integrity that I might not have had.

When I asked him if he would give me permission to write about his story, he said, "It's my life. I've got to take the good with the bad, and maybe it will help someone else get through what I went through." I hope he is right.

Most recently, he has faced another ordeal. His mother has ovarian cancer, and he has cared for her every step of the way as she has been near death and extremely sick from the chemotherapy. He has bathed her, dressed her, cooked for her, and been her constant companion. Through it all, I have never heard him complain.

Recently, as we were playing golf together as we often do, I remarked at how faithful he was in caring for his mother. Without hesitation he replied, "She never gave up on me when I gave her every reason to do so. The least I can do for her is pay her back a little now when she needs me."

It will soon be five years since Arthur's last recurrence of the cancer, but he will never be free of the possibility of its return. He has been drug free for even longer, but he knows that he can never let down his guard or he could be lost once again. Arthur came close to the edge twice in his young life, but somehow he emerged with a vision and love of life that he did not have before. This vision helps him care for his mother. It helps him care for the patients that we see every day. It is ironic that I now find it somewhat appropriate to think of the Church Health Center as being associated with Arthur Church. The way he has risen from the wounds and brokenness of the abyss makes me glad that he is one of us. By virtue of his suffering, we are better able to care for those who come to us with a sense of hopelessness. I can always point to Arthur and know what good things can arise out of despair.

What Makes Life Good

Mr. Farnsworth

"Quick, we need a doctor right now! He's having a seizure out in the van."

I could hear a woman's panic-filled voice. She was frantically trying to get my attention. Stan, our new medical assistant, also heard her cry and ran out to help. I dropped the chart I had in my hand and followed Stan out the back door.

It was a blistering summer day in Memphis. The temperature was in the high nineties, and there was only an occasional cloud in the sky. The heat hit me in the face as I rushed through the door. Parked along the side of our driveway was a fifteen-passenger van. It was old and battered. Its gray paint had been so sun-baked that it had a bluish hue to it. By the time we reached the van, the woman who had been driving and had sought our assistance had returned to the van.

"He's in the back!" she said. Without hesitation Stan and I rushed to the back of the vehicle and began fumbling with its back door which led to the rear seat. It wouldn't open.

"That hasn't worked for years," the woman told me. "You'll have to go through the side door." On the left side were two doors that faced each other. I reached for the one on the right.

"That one doesn't work either," she said. I quickly glanced at her then opened the one remaining door. It creaked open, but only about half-way.

As I stepped into the van, I immediately heard the sound of someone thrashing about in the rear seat. There were three seats I needed to climb over in order to get to him, and every seat was taken by a live human being. Each person sat facing forward as though nothing was happening—oblivious to the situation. No one was panicked, and no one seemed to notice that anything was out of the ordinary. It could have been a scene out of a Kafka novel or the movie *Dream Team*.

After assessing the situation, Stan and I began climbing over seats to get to the rear. We excused ourselves to every person we encountered, at which point they politely leaned to the side to let us pass.

When we finally got to the man who was having a seizure, he was beginning to stop his violent shaking. Stan and I tried to prevent him from hurting himself and waited for the episode to be over. After a couple of minutes, he stopped shaking and lay still but unconscious. At that point, I looked at Stan and asked, "Do you think we can get him out of here?"

Stan, who had been a sergeant in the Army and who regularly worked out with weights, responded, "Sure, Doc, no problem." I had my doubts.

Together Stan and I began lifting the man over the seats and aimed him toward the partially open door. All the passengers in the van once again politely leaned to the side as we passed and then returned to their positions facing forward.

I was not sure I was going to be able to hold the man up the entire way, but fortunately Stan's strength held up his half plus part of mine. When we got to the door, I was sweating bullets and my lab coat was torn in three places.

Just as we were able to stand again on firm ground and begin to carry the man into the health center, one of the women in the van leaned over and asked me, "Do you think we will be much longer?"

I shook my head and smiled and said, "It will be a few more minutes."

And so I met Mr. Marcus Farnsworth.

By the time we got him into a treatment room, he was starting to wake up. He lay on the table for a few minutes as I listened to his heart and the nurses began taking his vital signs and doing an EKG. By the time they were finished, he asked politely, "May I sit up now?"

"If you feel like it," I said.

He sat up on the side of the table and looked straight at me. He was a man in his late fifties, with salt and pepper hair and a day's growth of beard. He was wearing thick "Coke-bottle" glasses which were broken. He was slightly built and could not have weighed more than 130 pounds even though he was about five feet nine inches tall. He looked like a character from a Walter Mitty short story.

After a moment, he asked, "Can I go now?"

"Just a minute, Mr. Farnsworth. I'd like to talk to you about your seizures and see whether we can do something about them." I tried to be gentle as I spoke to him.

"Okay," he said. "But I've had them all my life."

As it turned out, Mr. Farnsworth had indeed had epilepsy all of his life, but he had not seen a doctor for it in several years and had not had any medicine for quite a while. He also had suffered from schizophrenia for more than thirty years, but he was not currently having problems with hallucinations or the usual problems of schizophrenia. He had reached a stage of his disease that is sometimes referred to as being "burned out."

At this point the driver of the van knocked on the door. She entered the room and introduced herself as Deloris. She was the caretaker for Mr. Farnsworth and the entire entourage in the van. Everyone lived together at the Faxon Group House, a shared living facility for people unable to care for themselves for whatever reason. Some were too difficult for a family member to look out for. Some were alone in the world with no one to help them. Mr. Farnsworth fell in the latter group.

Group homes like this are common in Memphis. They are cheaper than nursing homes and therefore popular among lower income families. These settings are also notorious for providing a very poor quality of care. Often the owner of the home packs as many people as possible into an old house and hires the cheapest staff he or she can get by with in order to maximize profits. The staff is often minimally trained and uncaring toward the residents. I could tell almost instantly this was not the case with Deloris.

As she walked into the room, Deloris began explaining to me that Mr. Farnsworth had an appointment to see me the next week. He was a new resident and she knew about his seizures, but she had not been able to get an appointment with us before then. She also knew he would not be able to afford his medicine. That's why she was bringing him to me. It was a coincidence that he had had a seizure while waiting in the van for me to see one of the other residents of Faxon Home.

"Deloris," I said, "why is everyone out there waiting in the van?"

"Well," she began. "I don't have a lot of help, and I can't just leave them alone at the house. So when someone needs to go to the doctor, we all go. I leave them in the van because most places can't handle it too well when we all walk in together. Plus, as I'm sure you've noticed, they are very patient when they sit there. No one minds too much about going."

I could see her dilemma, and from firsthand experience, I believed her when she said that the other residents did not mind sitting in the van, but I thought we could certainly make things more convenient by scheduling their appointments close together and on the same day. As I began to talk to her about how we could help, I realized that I was committing to be the doctor for Faxon Home, or at least for those residents who had no other physician to care for them. I knew it would be an interesting experience.

I started Mr. Farnsworth on anti-seizure medicines and asked to see him again in two weeks. But before everyone left, I had to see the patient who was the reason for everyone being there in the first place.

During all this time, Mary had been sitting in the waiting room. She was in her mid-twenties and, unlike Mr. Farnsworth, she was actively schizophrenic. She both heard voices telling her about the secrets of the universe and believed her body was being invaded by tiny aliens trying to infect her through her skin. In order to kill the aliens, she had sat in boiling hot water.

I'm not sure whether she "killed the aliens," but she did succeed in burning off the top layer of skin on her buttocks and the back of her legs. She seemed oblivious to the pain and was only concerned as to whether I thought her actions had accomplished their intention of killing the aliens.

"Yes, Mary," I said. "I do not think you have aliens invading your body, but I think we need to use this cream in order to keep them out for the next couple of weeks." It was the only thing I could think of to make sure she would use the cream to help heal her wounds and would not start thinking that I was trying to poison her with an alien concoction. She agreed to follow my instructions, and I repeated them to Deloris who listened closely and wrote them down.

As Mr. Farnsworth and Mary walked out the door with Deloris, I realized what a great sense of admiration and respect I had for Deloris. I could only imagine what it must be like to live and work with people like Mary, who had no basis in reality, and like Mr. Farnsworth, who was kind and gentle but unable to have a normal conversation. Deloris was plenty smart enough to have many other jobs, but she had a profound commitment to care for the unwanted. I made sure we tried to help Deloris whenever we could, and I was always glad to see patients from Faxon Home for brief periods of time when they came to me. But that was far different from looking out for their every need, every day.

Over the next several years, I got to know Mr. Farnsworth fairly well. He returned to the office often because of his seizures, and from time to time he had other health problems. When he came, I always tried to talk with him about his life, and he seemed to appreciate my interest in him.

Mr. Farnsworth usually had very little to say unless he was asked a direct question. When he came for his visits, he frequently had several small complaints, but he was usually satisfied with whatever answer I gave him regarding the treatment for his problems.

From that first day, I noticed that the plastic frames on his glasses were broken but he was content to hold them together with cellophane tape. One day when he came in, I saw that he had rigged his glasses so that a rubber band was hooked around his ear to hold them on. He realized this was not a good solution and agreed to have us help him get a new pair. He even seemed happy at the prospect and was in a good mood.

I talked to him for a few minutes about his life and how he spent his time at Faxon Home. While telling me that there was little that he longed for that he didn't have, he told me in a straightforward way how he spent his life.

"I am able to think about what makes life good, and then I try and live it."

He had no further commentary on these words of wisdom, and I returned to telling him about how to take his medicine and when I wanted to see him back again. He nodded his head to let me know he understood, then waited silently for the nurses to bring his prescriptions. I, however, continued to wonder how much I understood about the things that made life good and how to live in such a way as to make these things become reality.

Soon after this visit, for some reason, Mr. Farnsworth's appointments began being made with Dr. White instead of me. From time to time I would see Mr. Farnsworth in the pharmacy waiting area, and I would go out of my way to speak to him. He was always polite and called me by my name. I made certain he was happy with Dr. White, and he seemed to like him a great deal. Dr. White took care to look out for him in every way possible.

All seemed to stay on a steady course until one day when Dr. White showed me Mr. Farnsworth's chest x-ray. There was little doubt he had lung cancer. He had always smoked, and now his smoking had caught up with him. By the time the diagnosis was made, there was little that could be done. He began treatment for cancer, but every time I saw him, he had lost more weight and seemed a little sicker. But he took it all in stride.

One afternoon I was scheduled to have my picture taken for a local magazine. The photographer wanted more than just a snapshot of me seeing patients and instead had set up an elaborate array of lights in the foyer of our original building. I stood where I was supposed to stand and held my hands and head whichever way he told me to. This sort of thing is neither fun nor a choice but just a part of my job; such media coverage helps to publicize the work we do and helps us raise the money needed to continue.

As I stood on my mark, I was able to look through the glass window in the front door of the building. It was a bright, sunny day with only a few cars passing up and down the street. Then I saw Mr. Farnsworth slowly walking up the sidewalk. Without coming inside, he sat down on the steps of our building. He was not more than twenty feet in front of me.

Why is he alone? I wondered. It occurred to me that Deloris must have dropped him off for his visit with Dr. White, and he had returned to the place where she was to pick him up.

Did he notice me standing behind the door? I didn't think so. He looked to me to be at peace. I knew he was dying, but I wondered whether he fully grasped the seriousness of his disease.

While I was lost in thought about Mr. Farnsworth, John, the photographer, interrupted me, "Can you put your stethoscope around your neck and tilt your head a little to the right?"

I did as I was told but continued to watch Mr. Farnsworth. He looked straight ahead, only occasionally looking down the street to see if Deloris was coming. He did not appear anxious. Was he now thinking about the things that make life good? In the face of his own death, did he still find it possible to live in a manner that makes life worthwhile?

"Doctor, could you smile a little bit more and turn your head a little more toward me? Look right at the camera."

I tried my best to offer a big smile while my mind was racing with thoughts of a poor, schizophrenic man who had a peace and gentleness to him that I found extremely compelling. When I looked back out the window a few minutes later, he was gone. Deloris must have come while I was smiling at the camera. It was the last time I saw him.

A few weeks later, Debbie, one of the nurses, asked me, "Did you see Mr. Farnsworth's obituary in the newspaper? Apparently, he died in his sleep."

I had a sinking feeling in my stomach. How I wished that I had walked out and spoken to him on the last day that I had seen him! Suddenly I wished that I had told the photographer that I had something more important to do, at least for a moment. I wished I had smiled one last time at Mr. Farnsworth instead of at the camera. But I hadn't.

I have a picture in my mind of the absurdity of the first and last days I saw Mr. Farnsworth, but it has been the time in between that really sticks with me—the time during which I felt that I got to know him. Many people are afraid of schizophrenics and write them off as simply "crazy." I confess I have on occasion been guilty of such reactions myself. But Mr. Farnsworth was gentle and kind in ways that I don't think are part of my character. He was different. It's not that I wish I could be more like he was. I don't. I do wish, however, that I had a better feel for the secrets he learned about what makes life good.

"Please Don't Tell Mama"

Robert

"Doctor, you have to come help him. My baby is so pitiful. He's lying in that apartment with no electricity and no heat. He won't eat and he won't talk. You have to help me."

It was a cold November night, and I was the evening doctor at the clinic. I had received a telephone call from the mother of a patient I had gotten to know well. Robert, an African-American man in his early thirties, was dying of AIDS.

"Why have things gotten so bad?" I asked her.

"He's just refused to get any help for his cancer. He hasn't worked in almost a year, and he's got no money and won't take any help. Please come soon."

I could tell that Robert had not told his mother that he had AIDS. It was almost eight o'clock, and I had two more patients to see. I had been at the clinic since six o'clock that morning, and I was exhausted. I had only occasionally made house calls, and I knew there was nothing medically I could do for Robert.

"If you can bring him here in the morning, I can see him first thing," I told her.

"He won't come. Please come tonight. I don't know what else to do," she pleaded.

I paused for a moment, looking at the clock. Then I said, "I'll be there in an hour. Where is he?" She gave me the directions. Robert was living in an apartment in Hurt Village housing development. We have a number of patients who live in Hurt Village, but I had never been there. I experienced an immediate and unexpected adrenaline rush—pure fear. I was surprised and a little ashamed to find myself so frightened at the prospect of going to Hurt Village.

I hung up the phone. Before I could say anything, Stan said, "I'll go with you, Doc. I know that neighborhood real well. I've got a lot of friends who live around there."

When we arrived, the streetlights were out. It was dark, except for a single light on the corner of one of the buildings. As I got out of the car, I did not see anyone around. Then as my eyes adjusted to the darkness I noticed a group of young men standing in the shadows, watching us. A sense of threat and danger seemed almost palpable. I noticed I couldn't swallow and my palms were sweaty. I felt I had made a potentially costly error by wearing my white coat.

"Just keep walking," Stan whispered.

We walked along the sidewalk, looking for the building where Robert was living. We finally found it and headed up the stairs to the second floor. Several people passed us on the stairs, and there was a gathering of people talking quietly outside the door of Robert's apartment. As we approached, everyone fell silent.

"I'll get Mrs. Smith," someone said.

A few moments later a heavy-set woman in her late fifties made her way through the group and greeted us warmly.

"Oh, thank you, Doctor. Thank you, Jesus. I know you can make my Robert better." Tears were streaming down her face. "He's just lying there and won't eat. He's so weak. Please help him."

Stan and I entered the apartment. The apartment was cold, lit only by candlelight, and it smelled horrible. To my surprise the setting briefly reminded me of a past visit to a monastery, especially with several people standing in the room keeping vigil.

On a torn and soiled couch lay Robert, emaciated, weak, and dying. As I approached, he looked up at me and smiled. Chuckling he mumbled, "So, she made you come, too."

"I know there is nothing you can do," he continued. "I thought you might try one more time to get me to change my mind, but this time, I think it's too late."

Robert and I had had many conversations over the last couple of years about his disease. I had first gotten to know him right after the Church Health Center opened. At that time he was a brash and cocky young man. On his first visit to the Center he said, "You probably know me. I've got several radio programs, and I'm friends with some of your board members."

Whenever he came to the Center, he would usually tell us in great detail about his most recent encounter with some well-known person. At first he would come to the Center with minor complaints—colds, sore throats, and so on. Then one day he came in with a case of shingles. He told me that for several months he had had diarrhea. I was concerned he might be HIV positive.

"Robert, have you ever used drugs or done anything that might expose you to the AIDS virus?" I asked.

"A long time ago," he said. "When I was a teenager, I used drugs, but then I found Jesus and gave up all that stuff. There's no way I could have AIDS because God is looking out for me."

He resisted being tested for the virus, but I finally persuaded him to undergo the test. The results were positive. Robert refused to believe the diagnosis.

"No, there is no way that can be. I have claimed my healing. Doctor, I appreciate your concern about me, but I'll be okay."

Over the next year, it was all I could do to get him to accept the idea that he was indeed HIV infected. Even after he admitted the truth, he would not seek help or treatment.

Since he had no health insurance, he would logically have been treated at the city hospital's Adult Special Care Clinic—the Med's AIDS clinic. When I first suggested he go there, he quickly shot back, "I can't go there. I know too many people down there, and they might recognize me." Nothing I could say would persuade him to go to the Med.

Over the next several years, I saw Robert from time to time for various illnesses. He was always friendly and gradually became less and less egocentric. But he remained adamantly opposed to seeking any kind of treatment for AIDS. He would always say, "I have given my life to the Lord, and my life is in His hands."

"God does not want you to die, Robert," I would tell him. "God wants your life to be rich and full, and the doctors want to try to use the skills God has given them to help you have that life."

He would have none of it. On the occasions I would see him in the office, he would have an upper respiratory infection or a stomach virus or some other minor ailment, but never anything that required him to be in the hospital.

Then I did not see or hear from him for more than a year—not until the night his mother called me to come see him. As I looked at him lying on the couch, I could tell he was suffering terribly and had been for some time. He looked like he had lost more than eighty pounds. His face was drawn, and his eyes were sunken into his head. While I was talking with him, he leaned over and vomited into a bucket he kept by the couch. Then he tried to joke, "I can't seem to stop doing that."

I leaned over and stroked his back. "Robert, let us take you to the hospital. At least we can make you more comfortable there."

"No, Doc," he said. "I've made it this far with God's help. I just can't see going to the hospital now." He whispered, "Please don't tell Mama. She thinks I have cancer." I assured him I would not.

I sat down by the couch for a couple of minutes and then asked him if he needed anything. He shook his head and closed his eyes. After a few minutes, I stood and told Stan it was time to go.

As we walked out the door, Mrs. Smith came up to me and thanked me for coming. I took her hand and said, "I wish I knew a way to help him, but he doesn't want to go to the hospital. Please call me if he changes his mind or if I can be of help to you, Mrs. Smith."

She nodded, and Stan and I turned to leave. As we walked out, Robert's family and friends patted us both on the back. Then, at the last minute, a young woman ran up to me and said, "If he dies, what should we do about moving his body? I mean, because of his disease and all."

I paused, looked over at his mother, then said, "You mean, the cancer?"

The young woman looked at me quizzically and stammered, "Uh, yeah, the cancer."

"Just call the funeral home, and they will take care of everything," I said.

As we descended the stairs, I felt as though I were still in the room with Robert. I struggled with all I had just experienced—his suffering and the suffering of those closest to him, the deception about his disease, and his shocking living conditions. At the same time, I was strangely at peace. That darkened, candlelit room was filled with love and compassion—compassion from his mother and from his friends, but especially from Robert himself. I realized the gentle compassion and grace Robert showed me. He wanted to be my friend.

We reached the bottom of the stairs and started to walk to the car in the dark. I was jolted back to the immediate situation—the group of young men I had seen earlier were gathered beside my car. My heart raced. What would they do to us?

"How ya'll doing tonight?" Stan asked casually as we reached the car.

Several muffled voices responded, "All right."

Stan stepped past them toward the passenger door. I quickly opened the door on the driver's side and got in the car. The group watched as I unlocked Stan's door and he got in. I started the car. We locked the doors and drove away. Stan did not tell me about his own real fears for us both until we were back at the clinic.

Two days later, Robert's mother called me to tell me Robert had died.

"It was all so peaceful. He just went to sleep. God came and got him just like Robert wanted it to happen. Thank you for all your help, Doc." I hung up the phone and reflected on her expression of gratitude toward me.

I did not feel I had really done anything for Robert. I had not been able to persuade him to seek treatment for his disease. I could not even convince him to admit he had AIDS or to deal with it in some rational way. For a long time I had argued with him that he needed to seek further medical care. I even refused to believe with him that God was taking care of him. At every turn, I questioned his judgment and his beliefs.

Then I thought back on the feeling I had had when I had visited Robert two days earlier. At some deeper level, Robert and I had responded to each other, and we had won each other's trust. Robert had apparently realized this long before I could since I had been distracted by Robert's physical needs as my patient and had only   secondarily known him as person. Yet that feeling of being with Robert as he lay dying on the couch is one I will never forget. I find it to be a memory that has meaning I know can never be fully explored. In Robert's words, "I have claimed" it as a sacred moment.

"I Knew God Was Looking Out for Us"

Chicago Family

"I have a family here with two sick children. They have just arrived in Memphis. They have no money and don't know where they can take their kids. Do you think you can see them tonight?"

It was already 5:15 P.M.—almost time for the volunteer doctor to arrive, but he was an internist and did not treat children. I said, "Sure, if they can come right now, we can work them in."

"Thanks, Dr. Morris. I'll send them right over. I really appreciate your help," was the reply on the other end of the phone.

"No problem," I responded, hoping that the family would arrive quickly so I could get home at a decent hour.

I finished seeing my last scheduled patient and checked to see whether the family had arrived. I looked around the waiting room. No children. I went and worked on my charts, which needed to be reviewed.

About 30 minutes later I heard a baby crying. At last they had arrived.

The volunteer doctor had begun working, but the volunteer nurse and Arthur were free to get the children ready to see me. Within a few minutes Arthur came into the lab and said, "Doc, we're ready for you."

I immediately dropped what I was doing and walked into Room 4 where two small children, a man, and a woman were waiting for me.

As I opened the door, I noticed everyone looked a little harried. The children were two and four years of age, a boy and a girl respectively. The mother was holding Charlie, who seemed a little irritable. Rachel was busy opening drawers, at which point Roy, the father, said, "Stop that, or you'll be in trouble." She stopped.

I turned first to the mother, Julie, and asked what was wrong with Charlie.

"He's had a cold for a week and has had a fever for the last three days. I think he has an ear infection."

"Well," I said, "let's take a look."

Charlie fought me a little as I tried to look into his ears, but Julie lovingly held his hands. This allowed me enough of a glance to confirm the ear infection.

"You're right. Charlie does have an ear infection, but I think he'll get better soon once he starts taking the antibiotics I'm going to give him."

Roy broke in immediately.

"I'm afraid we don't have enough money to pay for any prescriptions." He looked sincere while Julie looked worried.

"It's okay," I tried to say gently. "We'll give you the medicine he needs here." They both looked relieved.

I then turned my attention to Rachel, who was again beginning to explore the exam room.

"Rachel," I called to her. "Come let me look at you." She stopped what she was doing and looked shyly at her mother.

"Go on," Julie said. "It's okay." Rachel walked over to me and stood with me. I reached out and put my arm around her back.

I have always loved the feeling of trust that a four- or five-year-old child can convey in a situation such as this. I am reminded of Jesus calling the children to him and his telling his followers to become like children. The innocence of a moment such as this with Rachel is what I suspect he intended us all to try to achieve.

As I looked at Rachel, I could tell she had a cold. Her nose was running, and she had a slight cough, but that was all. Otherwise she seemed healthy, except that she drew away from me when I touched her right arm.

"Ouch," she said.

"What happened there?" I asked her.

"She fell down while she was playing," Julie explained. "She'll be okay."

I reassured Julie and Roy that both children should be fine in a couple of days and that we would be happy to take care of them in the future if they did not have health insurance. Again, both parents seemed relieved.

I then asked, "I understand you've just come to Memphis. What brings you here?"

Roy, who was in his mid-twenties, unshaven, and wearing blue jeans, answered, "We left Chicago a week ago because my friend told us about jobs working in a hotel down here. We thought we might get a fresh start, but it hasn't worked out so well. We left last Monday, but our car broke down about the time we got to St. Louis. It took four days to get a new part, and all the money we had saved was used up. Then when we finally got here yesterday, we got to the hotel and they had gone and given the jobs to someone else because they thought we weren't coming."

By this time Julie had begun to cry softly while Roy continued. "Then two days ago, the kids got sick. Now here we are in Memphis, we don't know a soul, we got no job, no place to live, and to be honest, Doc, we got no money even to feed the kids tonight. We've spent the last two nights in the car. Today we went from church to church asking for help but without much luck. I guess you're sorry you asked."

I looked at my watch. It was seven o'clock. What was I supposed to do now? How could I give this family medicine for their sick children and then just send them on their way to sleep one more night in the car. Finally I said, "If you can wait for a few more minutes, I'll see what I can do."

I left the room to use the telephone. I began calling shelters I knew of, but everyone either was already full or not prepared to take a family. Finally, the Salvation Army agreed to give them a place for the night together, but they had already served dinner. I hung up the phone and heard the evening volunteer nurse say, "I couldn't help overhearing your conversation, and I might have an idea that will help."

"Go ahead," I said.

"Well, do you know of the P&H Cafe?"

I was familiar with the P&H. It is a Memphis institution although it's hard to describe. It's a cross between a bar, a nightclub, and a diner. I had been there a couple of times with friends, and I knew we had at least one patient who worked there as a waitress.

I encouraged the nurse to tell me her idea. She continued, "I've been told that the P&H will never turn anyone away who is hungry. Why don't you send them over there?"

It seemed worth a try. I picked up the phone and called. When someone answered, I could hear music in the background. When I identified who I was, the voice exclaimed, "Doctor Morris, this is Thelma. I'm one of your patients."

I knew immediately who she was. I told Thelma the story, and without hesitation she said, "Send them on down."

I went back into the room and told Roy and Julie what I had arranged. Their faces lit up, and they seemed very appreciative. Roy shook my hand and said, "I knew God was looking out for us when He sent us to someplace called the Church Health Center." I tried to hide my pride and told Roy that a number of people were involved in helping his family, but as they walked out the door, I could not help feeling a sense of achievement.

The next day, I called Thelma to see how things had gone with my family. As soon as I got her, she began to hoot, "You will not believe what happened!"

"What?" I said. "Tell me."

"It was incredible."

"Okay, Thelma, tell me!" I demanded.

She began, "They got here about ten minutes after I hung up talking with you, but it so happens that Leroy

James was sitting next to me, listening while I was on the phone with you. Do you know who he is?"

"I know," I answered. "He works at the Crown Plaza Hotel and he's a great supporter of the Church Health Center. So what does he have to do with anything?"

"He hears me talking to you, and knows that the family is looking for jobs in a hotel. After they come in and are about to finish eating, I watch him go up to them, give the man his card, and tell them that if they come down to the hotel tomorrow, he'll give them both a job. How about that, sports fans?"

I was stunned. "Thanks, Thelma, for your help. I'll see you at your next appointment." And I hung up.

The rest of the day I could not stop thinking about this series of events and how it all worked out. I began to wonder about the concept of providence. All of this could not have happened just by accident. I then thought about what an amazing story it was to tell people about the Church Health Center. It had all of the components I could possibly want: a family in great need who are helped by another patient, a volunteer nurse, and a financial supporter of the center. It seemed ideal—that is, until two weeks later when I learned the real truth about Julie and Roy.

It was a Tuesday morning. Nothing had happened out of the ordinary. The waiting room was packed, but things were going fairly smoothly until Kim came to me and said, "There is a woman out here with two small children who says she has to see you. She says she is from Chicago and you helped her and her children two weeks ago. What do you want me to do?"

I knew immediately who it was and at first thought that perhaps Charlie's ear infection had recurred, but I wasn't sure. I told Kim, "Work them in at the end of the morning. I'm not going anywhere at lunch time."

I was anxious to know why Julie was back. She was again in Room 4. When I opened the door, Charlie sat on Julie's lap and Rachel was clinging to her leg. Julie looked awful. She was a woman in her mid-twenties, attractive, with long brunette hair, but it was clear she had been crying and not sleeping.

I sat down on my stool and asked her softly, "What's the matter?" She blew her nose, and I asked naively, "Did the jobs at the Crowne Plaza not work out?"

She laughed a slight laugh, "We never even made it there the first day."

I was taken aback. "Why not?" I asked.

"Because of Roy," she said. "It's true we left Chicago to come to Memphis for a job, but our car never broke down. Instead, when we got to St. Louis, Roy met some guys at the truck stop, and they went off and smoked crack for four days. He spent every penny we had. When we finally got here, he was too high to go for the interview. So that's why we didn't get the jobs. But I can't take it anymore with how he treats the kids when he's that way. Rachel didn't fall and hurt her arm. Her father pushed her down. If ever I say anything to him, he starts in on me. I've got to get out, and I didn't know anywhere to turn except to you. You were nice to me and the kids the other night. I know you will help us. My family is in Indiana, and I just need to get bus fare to get back to them. Will you help us?" Her hands and her face were pleading desperately with me.

I was a doctor, not a social worker. Should I just give her the money? Maybe this was another con, but I didn't think so. I was quite upset with how their perfect little story had fallen to pieces. The perfect story wasn't even true.

Once again I left the room and made a few phone calls. The YWCA Wife Abuse Shelter was willing to help her sort things out and get started in the right direction. I told Julie, "I think they will help you. It's the best I can do."

She cried once again, with the children in her arms. She was a pathetic sight, and I felt useless in trying to help her. Her problems seemed beyond me. I had no pills that would solve her problem. Her problem was much bigger than a meal, a place to stay, or a job. It was fundamentally a problem of the spirit, and I could not really help her in the next fifteen minutes. I was hopeful the wife-abuse shelter would give her the support she needed.

I handed her the address and wished her luck. She thanked me for my help, then walked out the door with her two children by her side.

A week later, I heard that she found the money to get back to Indiana and had left with Charlie and Rachel. I have never heard from her since. I don't know the end of the story, and I have wondered what good we did, if anything, for this family. I am not sure if any of the things we did made any difference, but I do believe, or at least hope, that our presence did. When this family was desperate with two sick children and knew nowhere to turn, the churches of Memphis, through the Church Health Center, were there for them. And when Julie was on the verge of being without hope, she turned again to the Church Health Center for help, and, as best we could, we stood with her.

Should we have done more? Who is to say? This is not a happy story. There is no happy ending. I only take comfort in knowing that both times she came to me, I found time to see her and offer her my best advice. I do not know whether I should have done more.

"Will You Pray for Me?"

Elizabeth

Forty-two-year-old women do not have heart attacks, or at least that is usually the case. Elizabeth, however, was the exception to the rule. She and her husband, Bill, were living an average middle-class life trying to raise their two children in a suburb of Memphis when the unthinkable happened. Bill was working as the manager of a warehouse and Elizabeth as a secretary. She didn't smoke, didn't drink, and did not have a family history of heart disease. Most of her life she had been fairly healthy. Both of her children were delivered without problems; and, despite struggling to make ends meet, she seemed to have a pretty good life.

At an even five feet, she was fairly small in stature but had plenty of energy to keep her family together. She was always running from one thing to the next and at first did not think anything of suddenly getting out of breath one Friday night. Soon, however, she began having a crushing chest pain that she knew wasn't normal. She turned to Bill

and said, "I don't know what's going on, but I think I need
to go to the hospital." Bill was startled and realized something was badly wrong. He raced to the nearest emergency room and anxiously waited for the doctor to see
Elizabeth. It did not take long for the emergency room
physician to make the diagnosis. Matter-of-factly he told
Elizabeth, "I'm afraid you are having a heart attack, but
I've called a heart surgeon and he is on the way." The idea
of a heart surgeon frightened Elizabeth and Bill, but in the
panic of the moment, they were willing to go along with
anything that needed to be done.

Within a few hours Elizabeth had a cardiac catheterization
and the cardiologist and cardiovascular surgeon both agreed
that she needed an immediate heart by-pass operation.
Elizabeth didn't know what to do. "I was afraid I was going
to die." So she signed the papers, and the surgery began.

For three anxious hours Bill and the children waited for
the surgery to be over. It was an enormous relief when the
surgeon came in the room and said, "Everything went very
well. She's in the recovery room now and she's going to be
fine." Bill took a deep breath and thanked God for sparing
Elizabeth's life.

For the next 24 hours everything went according to
schedule. She was taken off the ventilator and began to
breathe on her own. She was young, so everyone expected
her to recover quickly. But 24 hours after the surgery,
Elizabeth began having a sharp pain in her right leg. The
surgeon came to see her. The pulse in her right leg was
absent. Something was blocking the blood supply to her
right leg, causing the pain. He gave her a blood thinner
and waited until the morning to decide if she would need

any additional surgery. When morning came, the pain was no better. In fact, it was now also in her left leg, and the pulse on the left side was also absent.

The surgeon knew he had a big problem. He decided to take her back to the operating room. He tried repeatedly to open the obstructed arteries without success. In order to save Elizabeth's life, he had only one option. He swallowed hard and began the procedure. One by one he amputated Elizabeth's legs at the hip. She was never going to walk again, and her life was forever changed.

When she woke up, she still had the pain in her legs. She tried to move her legs to get some relief. There was no response. Then she looked down and saw what had happened. How could this be? How could God have done this to her? She began to cry. Bill reached out to hold her hand. What was happening was happening to both of them and to their whole family.

After weeks in the hospital, Elizabeth was discharged to go home. She tried to remain as upbeat as possible for the children, but life was hard. Everything had changed. She could not do the simplest of things without help. She couldn't drive; she couldn't even maneuver her wheelchair through the house. They never expected they would need their home to be handicap accessible. She could no longer work, so their income was cut in half. Thankfully, Bill's insurance paid for almost all of her hospital and doctor bills; but as a result, she used up her lifetime medical benefits. She still had health insurance, but it was essentially of no benefit to her.

It soon became a financial struggle to pay for all of her medicine. She had survived the heart attack, but it was clear she had significant disease that would continue to require care and treatment. How would they pay for all of this in the future? At first, Bill's employer was sympathetic to his plight. But after a while he became less willing to let Bill off early to take Elizabeth to the doctor. Bill tried not to let the stress he felt show through, but Elizabeth knew it was there.

For almost a year they did the best they could to make ends meet, but they kept falling further and further behind. The medical bills started to mount. Elizabeth applied for TennCare, Tennessee's version of Medicaid, but she got turned down. You cannot receive TennCare if you have another type of health insurance. It did not matter that she had used up her lifetime medical benefits. She had health insurance; therefore, she did not qualify for TennCare.

In time, someone told Elizabeth and Bill about the Church Health Center. They made an appointment—they had nothing to lose.

The first time I met Elizabeth I was afraid I could not handle all that would be involved in taking care of her. I, of course, immediately recognized that she had both legs amputated at the base of her torso, but I tried to pretend that this is something I see every day, which it is not. The day of her initial visit was a busy one in the clinic, but I tried to listen carefully to this tragic story. Elizabeth calmly told me about the series of events as she looked at me through her plastic-rimmed glasses that kept sliding down her nose. Her hair was black with streaks of gray, and I could tell that she had never been a very big woman. Now she seemed no larger than a small child.

As Elizabeth talked, Bill listened intently and would occasionally, very kindly, correct her version of the story.

He seemed very devoted. Her biggest physical problem that first day seemed to be persistent phantom pain. She perceived that the pain in her legs was still present even though the legs had been amputated over a year before. There is fairly effective medicine for this problem, which I noticed she was not on. I thought to myself, "At least I can help in some way." The bigger problems were all related to adjusting to this change in life. There was never enough money. Elizabeth couldn't drive. Bill's boss now only grudgingly let him off, and Elizabeth was very sad.

I knew of a church group called SOS, that helps fix up houses, so I hoped the group might help make this family's house handicap accessible. We could supply most of her medicine. That was the easy part. I encouraged her to come see Ron, our pastoral counselor, to which she readily agreed. And then, Bill very shyly asked me, "Do you think you can do something about her rocking?"

All through the interview I noticed that Elizabeth sat in her wheelchair and rocked back and forth. For over 20 minutes the rocking never stopped. To be honest, in just a few minutes I had come to find the constant sound very irritating and thought of asking him, "Why don't you just put on the wheelchair's brake?" Thankfully I did not say that.

As I thought about his question, Merilyn knocked on the door. "Dr. Morris, you have a phone call." I was glad to take the call as I thought about Bill's question. When I finished the call, I saw our pastoral counselor out of the corner of my eye and decided to tell him about Elizabeth. After quickly telling her story, I asked, "Ron, what do you make of the rocking?"

He thought for a minute and then replied, "You know, when people rock like that it usually means they want to be held." They want to be held! This was such a simple idea, but I suspected it was true.

I went back into the room, and without giving Ron credit, I said to them, "This has been a terrible ordeal for you both. I'm sure much of the time you feel like you only have each other. Maybe the rocking will get better if you can comfort Elizabeth by physically holding her more often."

At that point, Elizabeth began to cry. "It hasn't been the same since the surgery. I think he thinks he might break me."

Bill reached over and took Elizabeth into his arms and began to pat her back. "I love you as much as ever. I just haven't known what to do." That was the last time I ever saw Elizabeth rocking.

It was not, however, the last time I saw Elizabeth. Since that day I have seen her every two or three months and more often if she gets sick. Many of her social problems have persisted. There is still not enough money. She still does not qualify for TennCare, and she still cannot drive. Her children have grown up; and her daughter, Julie, got married when she was 19 and had a baby. Unfortunately the marriage lasted only a short while, and now she and the baby are back living with Elizabeth and Bill.

This past summer Elizabeth began complaining again of pain in her legs. I thought at first that this was her phantom pain again, but it was not exactly the same. The pain became increasingly intense. I began worrying that she might have a problem with her kidneys. I did an ultrasound that showed her right kidney was blocked. Why was this happening? Did she have a kidney stone? Or was it something worse? I arranged for her to go see a specialist the Monday after her appointment, which was on a Thursday afternoon. That afternoon Elizabeth said that the pain was better but she was afraid. "Dr. Morris, I just don't know what's happening to me. I've never had anything like this before. I know I've not asked you to do this before, but will you pray for me?"

Elizabeth knew that I am a Methodist minister as well as a family practice physician. I was glad to offer a prayer for her, and at the same time I was praying for wisdom to know how to diagnose and treat her problem. Before I began the prayer, Elizabeth reached her hand up and grabbed the back of my neck. She lifted herself up close to my face and closed her eyes. I reached out and took her hand and prayed softly. "God of all grace and kindness, let your healing hand touch your child Elizabeth, and may she feel your comfort and love in this moment and in the days to come."

She lowered herself back down into her wheelchair and I squeezed her hand. "Things will get better. Call me over the weekend if anything gets worse." She thanked me, and I wheeled her to the pharmacy waiting area.

The next morning Merilyn told me, "We got a call from the hospital. They admitted Elizabeth last night. Apparently the pain got worse and Bill took her in. They wanted you to know."

I started kicking myself mentally, wondering if I should have acted quicker. "At least now," I thought, "we can get to the bottom of the problem."

Early Saturday morning I went to the hospital to check on Elizabeth. As I walked into the room, there was Bill sitting in a chair by Elizabeth's bed, holding her hand. He had a worried look on his face but brightened up when he saw me. "She knew you would come," he smiled. "She had a rough night, but now she's sleeping."

I turned to him and in a hushed tone began to praise him. "You have been a wonderful husband to her; I hope you know that. No matter what happens, I see you sticking beside her because your love for her shines through."

He nodded his head. "She's all I've got and she means the world to me." I patted him on the back and then walked over to talk to Elizabeth. She appeared to indeed be asleep, but I wanted to ask her a few questions. I gently shook her shoulder. She did not respond. I shook a little harder. Still no response. I began to be alarmed. I opened her eyes, and she stared blankly ahead. She was not just asleep—she was in a coma!

I tried not to alarm Bill, but I raced out of the room and found the intern on the floor who was working with Elizabeth. I told him what had happened and asked him to call Dr. Miller, my friend who is the director of the residency program. I knew he was the attending physician for the weekend. Within a few minutes the whole resident team was in Elizabeth's room. A bed in the intensive care unit was made ready, and within 30 minutes Elizabeth was in the ICU, struggling for her life.

All of this happened so quickly that I am sure Bill did not know what to think. Within an hour her breathing was very shallow, so she was intubated and put on a ventilator. I talked to Bill and told him, "Things are happening very rapidly. It's not at all clear what is going on, but we have the best doctors helping and we will do all we can. Right now it does not look very good. I think you need to call the family together." The tears began to well up in Bill's eyes. I continued to talk to him, then put my arm around his shoulder and was quiet. There was nothing else to say.

Elizabeth's condition did not change for the next three days. The urologist put in tubes, known as stints, to drain her kidneys of the urine that was backing up, and she was put on kidney dialysis. She was stable, but she was still in a coma and the outlook was bleak. I talked to Bill every day—sometimes at work and sometimes in the hospital. He remained optimistic but I knew he was confused. Despite a covey of doctors, no one knew why she was so sick or what was wrong with her kidneys. Then, as quickly as it all began, Elizabeth began to get better. She came off the ventilator and began sitting up in bed. They were able to stop the dialysis. She was transferred out of the ICU and into a regular room.

When I was finally able to talk to her, her spirits were holding strong. "I almost died, didn't I?" she asked me.

"Yes, ma'am, but you didn't. It looks like you've still got more left to do."

She stayed in the hospital for another week. None of the doctors were able to figure out what had caused the problem in the first place, but she was now better. The stints were still in position, but the blockage in the kidney was gone and the pain was much better.

A week after she got out of the hospital, Elizabeth came to the office to see me. I was anxious about what I would tell her about her latest brush with death. She asked me to repeat for her all the series of events, which I did as best I could recall them. She then asked me, "Do you remember what we did the last time I was here just before I went into the hospital?"

How could I forget? It was etched into my memory. I slowly nodded my head and said, "I prayed for you." The room was silent. My mind began to race and I thought, "What would I have thought if I asked someone I trusted to pray for me and within 24 hours I was in a coma at death's door? I'm sure the thought would have passed through my mind,'What kind of God is this I believe in?'" My faith would have been shaken to the core.

As the silence lengthened, Elizabeth reached out and took my hand. Then with the utmost sincerity and with an expression of wonder, she said, "What might have happened if we had not had that prayer?"

My mind went blank. I thought about her question. What might have happened? I had no response, but I was filled with admiration for this tragic woman's faith. I knew that I did not have such a sense of assurance that God is looking out for me. I felt humble in her presence and in her belief in the miracle of God's presence in our lives.

Since that day Elizabeth has continued to struggle. The longer her daughter lives with her and Bill, the more tension exists between mother and daughter. There are unpaid bills from her long hospitalization which we are trying to have people forgive, but there is still not enough money to go around just for necessities. Still, Elizabeth clings to a faith that will not go away, that will not give up, that will not be replaced by bitterness and disappointment.

When Elizabeth comes for an appointment, no matter how busy I am, I make time to listen to whatever she wants to tell me. There is little I can do for most of her problems. But no matter what the reason for the encounter, every time I see her I can sense her hand upon my neck and feel her breath upon my cheek. What might have happened if we had not had that prayer? I'm glad I will never need to know the answer.

"What is Cancer?"

Igor, Tanya, and Miguel

Igor came to the walk-in clinic because his skin had recently turned yellow and his friend at work thought that he had contracted hepatitis. But it was soon clear that his problem was much worse than either of them suspected. Igor was a native of Poland. He had been in America for three years and in Memphis for four months. He left Poland, his wife, and family because his job in the coal mines did not pay enough to support the family. He came to America, like many economic refugees, seeking a better life. His 15-year-old son came with him, and they both began working wherever they could find a day's wage. What money he could, he saved and sent back home. Things were not the way he had dreamed they would be, but he still had hope.

Someone told Igor the job market was better in Memphis, so he packed his bags and he and his son came south. He began working two jobs, one as a dishwasher, the other as a laborer for a landscaping firm.

Soon after coming to Memphis he developed diarrhea. He tried to ignore it. He thought it would go away, but it didn't. He kept working but he began losing weight, a symptom he attributed to the diarrhea. "It must be something in the food or the water," he thought. He began getting weaker, but he kept working.

People at work noticed the problem when Igor became jaundiced. His skin and his eyes turned yellow, and they became worried he had contracted hepatitis. There had recently been an outbreak of hepatitis in Memphis, and the disease had received a lot of media attention. His friends, very alertly, insisted that he see a doctor.

Igor, of course, knew he was sick, but he also knew he did not have the money to pay a doctor. Plus, he had to keep working so he could send money back home to his family. Someone at work knew about the Church Health Center and brought Igor to our walk-in clinic on a morning when I was the doctor on duty.

When I first saw Igor, I was struck by how pleasant he was. He had a kind smile, but his eyes were sunken and his temples were wasted, as happens when someone is very sick. He greeted me in English, but after a few words, it was clear we were going to have a language problem.

When I was in college, I spent my junior year in London, where I had a Polish friend. She had tried to teach me a little of the language, but I was never very good. I could not roll my "R"s properly. When I tried to say, "Hello, how are you?" with my tongue-tied pronunciation, it always came out in translation, "Hello, how did you commit suicide?" Despite my eager attempts to learn the language, she and I agreed that it would be better if we spoke English.

I did not try to say anything to Igor except hello. Whenever we came to an impasse, he would turn to a Polish-English computer he carried with him. He took great care of his "machine." He kept it in a Styrofoam case and never took it out. It was clear that he had used it a great deal, because the edges of the Styrofoam were worn. Fortunately, the case had prevented the machine from being broken.

Unfortunately, the translator could work with only one word at a time. Although it was better than nothing, it was very frustrating to use.

I explained to Igor that we would need to do tests to make a diagnosis of his condition, but after feeling his abdomen, I was already fairly sure of the cause. His liver was greatly enlarged and was rock hard. I felt certain he had some form of cancer; it only remained to determine what kind and how advanced it was.

I continued to smile at Igor, even though I feared the worst and was already trying to figure out how we could take care of him. He was an immigrant who had no family with him other than his son, no insurance, very little money—and he spoke only a few words of English. If he did have cancer, what were we going to do? What was best for him, and how could we arrange to get him the treatment he needed?

This was not the first time I had faced such a dilemma. This has been a recurring problem for the last twelve years as refugees and undocumented workers have found their way to our door, sick and alone, without health insurance, without command of the language, and therefore with little chance of finding a good job.

One of the first such dilemmas I faced occurred during the first year we were open and also involved a native of Poland. Tanya was the mother of two children—one an energetic five-year-old girl and the other a playful ten-year-old boy named Lech. When I first met the family, everything seemed normal except that Lech's head was completely bald. I quickly realized the problem: Lech was suffering from leukemia and was a patient at St. Jude Children's Research Hospital in Memphis. This well known hospital was started in 1962 by Danny Thomas. They do research and treat children with severe childhood illnesses, including cancers such as leukemia. St. Jude is extremely generous with its resources and never refuses to treat a child because of an inability to pay, provided the family can arrange to get the child to Memphis.

Such was the case with Lech. His father was a low-level government official in the Polish Communist party. He made an adequate living by Polish standards, but very modest by ours. Tanya was a chemist with a Ph.D. and worked at a university. Her salary was also very modest despite her advanced education. Between the two of them, they saved enough money to bring Lech to Memphis once they heard of the successful treatment that was being done at St. Jude. St. Jude's success rate was far greater than anything being achieved in Poland. Getting the appropriate visas for the children and Tanya was not difficult, but the father chose to stay home in order to keep his job. Tanya left her home, with the two children, to venture to the great unknown of Memphis, Tennessee.

When they first came, Lech was very sick, and the family was caught up in the intensity and all-consuming nature of caring for a child on the verge of death. Fortunately, Lech responded quickly and dramatically to the treatment and within weeks was acting like a normal ten-year-old. That's when the new problems began.

Because St. Jude is a research hospital, Lech was randomized to a treatment protocol which would require three years of follow-up and outpatient treatment. This meant staying in Memphis the entire time. Tanya could risk returning to Poland for the treatment but she could not be certain that the same drugs would be available, and she would not be around the doctors who saved her child's life. She made the decision almost any mother would make: She decided to stay in Memphis.

While the Immigration Service was willing to let the family stay, what they did not grant her was a work permit. She could live in Memphis but she could not work in Memphis. It would be up to the father to support the family on his wages from his job in Poland.

Tanya did all she could to live frugally. She rented an apartment in a very undesirable part of town because it was only $180 a month. The social workers at St. Jude helped as much as they could, but this was not the first time this problem had occurred, and their resources to help consisted mostly of encouraging words. Over the past twelve years we have seen many families from around the world in this same predicament. In fact, the Church Health Center has, on an informal basis, become the doctor's office for international families who have a child with a life-threatening disease at St. Jude. They take care of the leukemia; we take care of the strep throat. In fact, many of the St. Jude doctors volunteer on our pediatric nights, and we joke together at how they enjoy seeing "well children." It's a relationship that has been good for all of us.

For Tanya and her children, living frugally soon became living in poverty. Tanya applied for a work permit but was turned down. She wrote to our congressman but did not get a reply. She didn't know what to do. She had a Ph.D. in chemistry, was willing to work, but could not even look for a job. She knew it was illegal, but her children came first: She began cleaning houses. And cleaning houses was what she was doing when I first met her.

As I became Tanya and Katya's doctor, I slowly learned the story I have just outlined. Something about it did not seem right. It didn't seem like the American way. I took it upon myself to see if I could help her get a work permit. After many calls, I was told she would first need to find an employer willing to hire her, and the prospective employer would have to petition for the permit. Not to be deterred, I set out to find the employer.

Fortunately, a vice-president of Schering-Plough, John Clayton, was a member of our board. This is a large pharmaceutical company which makes many products ranging from St. Joseph's aspirin to suntan lotion to prescription drugs. What I suspected was that they employed a lot of chemists, and I was right.

Thanks to John's perseverance, Schering-Plough was willing to give Tanya a chance and was also willing to fill out the forms. Finally it seemed like all would work out. Then one day Tanya came to me with tears in her eyes. She showed me her letter denying her request for a work permit. She looked at me and said, "Why they do this?" I did not have an answer.

At that point, I made my first foray into politics beyond the Memphis City Council. Another board member and a member of my church, Joy Tiffin, was then-Senator Al Gore's Memphis representative. I called Joy and asked for her help. She talked to their attorney, Greg Duckett, and together they told me that they thought "Al" could help. Tanya and I both waited for an answer. Nothing in government works fast, but six weeks later Tanya came to me all smiles. "I got my work permit." It was a great relief, and I felt a sense of satisfaction.

Several months later, after Tanya was working successfully in her job, she appeared without an appointment to introduce me to her husband. The Make-A-Wish Foundation had chosen Lech as a child whose wish they would grant. They flew his father to Memphis from Poland, and now all of the family was being taken to Disney World! As thanks for my small part in helping the family, the father had hand-carved a chess set for me. It was a wonderful gift and still sits in my office today. My memories of Tanya rushed through my mind as I sat before Igor thinking of what to say.

Igor hung on every word as I began to tell him of my plan to make a diagnosis and begin treatment. I made it clear that he was a very sick man, a concept that somehow seemed to take him by surprise. He seemed certain that if he only took a few pills, he would be back at work feeling like his usual self. After all, he was only 45 years old.

I told him of the need to first get a CAT Scan, a fancy x-ray that could look inside his body. I tried to explain the procedure, but I was having difficulty finding words he understood and the translator took too long. I finally left it at "Trust me, it doesn't hurt." That seemed to be good enough.

Two days later he returned to go over his results. The report of the CAT Scan was worse than I had thought, and the laboratory values were equally bad. The tumor had spread throughout his liver, and there were multiple growths in his lungs as well. It was still uncertain in what organ the cancer had begun, but a second-year medical school student could tell you that the prognosis was very poor no matter what.

I was faced again with the question of what we could do, medically, to care for a man from Poland without insurance, who seemed to be dying. I called one of the health center's best friends, Dr. Lee Schwartzberg, an oncologist who volunteers both as a specialist and as a primary care physician. Despite being Jewish, Lee believes in the work of the Church Health Center. People are often surprised to learn how much Jewish support we have, considering I am a Methodist minister, our name has the word "church" in it, and our logo has a cross in the middle. To answer the question, "Why should Jews support the Church Health Center?" one of my best friends, Rabbi Micah Greenstein, has often quoted Elie Wiesel by saying, "Being Jewish is not about making the world more Jewish, it is about making the world more human." Micah goes on to say, "That is exactly what the Church Health Center is doing, and for that reason, every Jew in Memphis should support it." I have never discussed the issue with Dr. Schwartzberg, but I am sure that is the way he also feels.

As for Igor, after I told Dr. Schwartzberg my findings, he was very discouraging. He told me that we needed a definite diagnosis, which we would get by doing a biopsy; but even in the more optimistic scenarios it was unlikely he would live more than six months. Dr. Schwartzberg volunteered to help care for him once the diagnosis was made, so at least I now had an oncologist to help with the care if I needed it.

Armed with this awful news, I opened the door and sat down to talk with Igor. His friend from work was again with him. I could tell he was hanging on my every word. I have long ago come to believe that it is best to tell patients the truth and to tell them all I know as soon as possible, so I proceeded to tell Igor what I believed was the cause of his illness. I told him that the result of the CAT Scan was not good news, that he most certainly had cancer.

He looked at me with a blank face. "What is cancer?" he said. He slid his translator toward me. I paused for a moment with a sick feeling that I was going to have to type in C-A-N-C-E-R. I looked at his friend who understood my anguish at what was about to happen. I reached for his computer and typed in the word and then hit "enter." Igor stared at the translation and then said, "I'm a dead man." I tried to reassure him, but what could I say? How could I console him? I hardly knew him, and we did not speak the same language. I could sense his feeling of aloneness.

He asked me what his chances were. "If zero percent, I go to Poland," he said. I could not tell him zero percent, so I said ten percent: There is always a chance for a miracle. He then turned to me and looked in my eyes. "Should I go to Poland?"

We sat in silence for a few seconds while I pondered what to say. It seemed the right thing to do. I said, "Yes, go to Poland."

But before he went we needed a definite diagnosis— something to tell the doctors in Poland when he got there. In order to have a diagnosis, he needed to have a biopsy done. I called Dr. Steve Miller, the director of what is known as the Methodist Teaching Practice, the residency training program for Methodist Hospital. Both the hospital and the offices of the Teaching Practice are only a few blocks from us. Dr. Miller has become a close friend and is always willing to help care for our patients, especially when they need to be admitted to the hospital. I told him Igor's story and he quickly said, "Have him come tomorrow, and we will get the biopsy done." This was a great relief.

I told Igor the plan, and he seemed resigned. His friend was willing to go with him the next day.

I can only imagine how frightening it must be to be a foreigner in the United States and become sick and have to access our health care system. For many, the fact that we do not have universal health care is at first a surprise and then a shock, especially when they learn how much it can cost. During the year I was living in England, my foot was accidentally run over by a car. Thankfully, it was a very small sportscar. While I was not seriously injured, it was necessary for me to go to the hospital for treatment. At no point was I charged for the care given me, even though I had good health insurance. Although I was not British, I was given good care without regard for the cost.

In this country, immigrants quickly learn that an inability to pay may drastically limit their options unless they have a life-threatening injury or disease. I have often seen refugees bewildered by the lack of government-supplied universal health care. More common still is their shock at the cost of health care even in those situations when the immigrant is prepared to pay.

Miguel and his wife, Maria, came to the United States primarily so that Miguel could receive better health care for his problem. Ten years before, Miguel was in a diving accident, which left him paralyzed from the waist down and with only limited use of his arms. At the time, they were living with their two children in a small village in Mexico. The local hospital gave Miguel the best care they had to offer, but it was limited in scope. Maria took care of him as well as she could, but she did not have any training; she just did what seemed right. Over the years, Miguel developed very large pressure sores on his buttocks from sitting in a wheelchair all day long. As the sores got larger and larger, Maria became more and more concerned about her husband. The local doctors did not know what to do. She decided his only help would come by going to the United States.

The family, however, did not have the money and could not get the right immigration papers to make the trip. After much agony, Maria left her family and crossed the border illegally into Texas. She had friends who were living in Memphis who promised to help her if she could get here.

She hitchhiked to Tennessee, found her friends, and began sleeping on their couch. She spent all of her time learning English, and within a few weeks, she was able to get by enough with the language to find a job working as a waitress in a local Mexican restaurant.

She caught on fast and did well. For a year and a half she worked as many hours as she could to save the money she would need to pay to sneak Miguel and her children into the country. Finally, she was able to send the money home, and Miguel set out to cross the border.

I have seen a number of TV programs which show Mexicans crossing the Rio Grande at night. The terrain is hard and the journey is fraught with danger. I was not told how Miguel, a paralyzed man with two small children, made the trip, but I suspect the crossing was tortuous and expensive. But finally the family was reunited.

At last Miguel could receive the treatment he needed to care for his wounds, or so they thought. When Maria tried to arrange for an appointment to see a specialist in wound care, she could not even afford the cost for the first visit, much less the ongoing cost of treatment. She tried to make an appointment at the city hospital, but since Miguel did not have a Social Security card and was not a resident of Shelby County, he could not be seen.

What was she to do? After years of effort, she had managed to bring him to the water of life, or so she imagined, yet the fountain could not be turned on for her family. The despair must have been great.

Other Mexican friends told her about the Church Health Center, so she took a chance on bringing him to our door. His appointment was made with me. Both Maria and Miguel were pleasant and polite during our first visit. She translated for me and slowly told me of their ordeal.

After I heard her story, the time came to look at his wound. With some effort we were able to get him on the table. While Maria was away from the family, there had not been anyone to care for Miguel in more than a cursory way. He did the best he could to look after the children, but his arms did not function well enough for him to care for his wound.

I was not prepared for what I saw. There was a hole on his bottom that a grapefruit could easily fit into. This was not an everyday pressure sore and would need much specialized care. What was I to do?

I knew that over the years I had developed a network of volunteers and donated services to provide the care that Miguel needed. But to do so would eat up a lot of good will and mean I could not go back to those volunteers for a while. Was it right to use those resources on someone who was an illegal alien, when I knew that if someone from south Memphis came with a similar problem the next week, I might have trouble offering the same quality of care? In addition, would it matter to any of the volunteers that both Miguel and Maria were illegal aliens? I was sure that some of the people who would be treating him would take a hard stance on tightening the border with Mexico, and I wondered if they would be angry with me for sending them someone I knew was "illegal."

I have thought more about this dilemma since I first saw Miguel, but at the time I did not ponder long on the problem. When faced with the size of his ulcer, I quickly began to formulate a plan and tried to figure out all of the doctors and services we would need to help heal his wound. Within a few minutes the plan was made, and the nurses were explaining to Miguel and Maria what would happen next.

I resolved this dilemma quickly because while I was in seminary, I once heard Henri Nouwen tell how Thomas Merton always believed that one has a moral obligation to care for the suffering individual who is in his presence. No other obligation ranks higher. It seemed to me that Miguel fit this situation. No matter what the consequences might be or what his immigration status was, I was bound to do what I could to help ease his suffering. That reasoning made sense to me at the time and still does today.

My decision to use our resources to help Miguel made it easier to use the same logic with Igor. So I was glad when I learned that he had kept his appointment with the teaching practice the next day. He arrived scared, but resolute in his desire to know what he was facing, and still slightly hopeful that maybe I was wrong. In order to do the biopsy, he was placed on the CAT Scan table again. After an image of his liver was generated, the radiologist slowly pierced his skin and placed a needle into a piece of the large tumor growing there. When the needle was withdrawn, a piece of the tumor came along, and it was sent to the laboratory. Looking under the microscope did not reveal good news: Igor had a very aggressive form of colon cancer which had spread to both his liver and his lung. The prognosis was close to zero percent.

Igor began making plans to return to Poland, but the doctors wanted to keep him in the hospital for a couple of days to begin whatever treatment they could on the tumor. I have little doubt that he was scared, but he agreed to the plan. After the first day in the hospital, Dr. Miller called to tell me what the plan was. He also told me that one of the residents could speak Polish and a pharmacist spoke

Russian, so they could at least communicate with Igor. And, he told me, one of the social workers was working on plans to get him home to Poland.

Four or five days went by before I saw Dr. Miller again. We were at a meeting discussing future plans for the health center. When the meeting was over, he very calmly told me, "Igor died."

I responded with stunned silence and then asked, "What happened?"

"His liver just gave out," he said.

But I could not help wondering, "Did he instead decide that the battle was not worth it and so he simply gave up?"

I know that there is little else I could have done to help Igor. But my experiences with him, Tanya, and Miguel have taught me that the world is indeed very small, and that God's love for God's children extends beyond any national borders. I now know in my heart that Henri Nouwen and Thomas Merton were right. Whomever I meet, no matter what the circumstance, is my neighbor. And the Golden Rule always applies. I must love my neighbor as myself. There are no exceptions.

Willie and Easter

"You girls sure are looking good today. It seems like every time I come over here you get prettier and prettier." That was a comment I had heard Willie Green make on more than one occasion.

"Oh, Mr. Green, you must be getting blind as you get older," was Debbie's response to his somewhat flirtatious remark. I had overheard other male patients say similar things to the nurses, and all of them were dealt with in a quick, at times curt manner directed toward getting the conversation back on a professional level immediately. But they allowed Willie Green to get away with saying things that no one else could. I'm not quite sure why that was, except it always seemed clear that he was simply trying to brighten everyone's day.

Willie was tall, almost six feet five inches, lean and rugged. He always wore work clothes and usually had at least a day's growth of beard. He walked with a loping gait, and he usually wore a baseball cap, which he held in his hands whenever he was inside. I especially remember his hands. They were huge—twice the size of mine and covered with thick, rough calluses.

He would come to the clinic four or five times a year, usually because of his high blood pressure or a cold or sore throat—never anything serious. Then one day he showed up at the clinic, and he seemed completely different; he had developed a racing heartbeat and was suffering shortness of breath.

"Doc, I think my ticker's gone haywire, and whenever I breathe I feel like I've swallowed a canary." He was clearly in trouble. When I listened to his heart, I could tell right away he was in atrial fibrillation, an irregular heartbeat which is often not serious but which, at times, can be life threatening. His difficulty in breathing was because his heart was beating so fast and so ineffectively.

"Willie," I said, "you're going to have to go to the hospital."

"Now, Doc, you know I don't have any money. Can't you just give me a pill, pat me on my back, and send me on my way?" He was anxious, but he still had a twinkle in his eye.

"Sorry, Willie. I wish I could make everything better right here, but I think you're going to need a couple of days in the hospital," I said, trying to reassure him.

He shook his head, "Well, why should I come to the doctor if I am going to remain thick-headed just like I've been all my life? Just call for the hearse, I mean ambulance, and haul me away." He smiled a weak smile.

Within a few days his symptoms were resolved, but the cardiologist had not been able to get his heart rate back into a normal rhythm. He remained in atrial fibrillation. This condition is normally not a serious problem as long as the patient stays on a blood thinner.

After his stay in the hospital, Willie came every month to the clinic to get his blood drawn in order to check to see if the blood thinner was working appropriately. Sometimes I never actually saw him but could hear his voice and the laughter of the nurses when he was there.

"Who is going to bite me on the neck today to get my blood? Just be careful, I haven't eaten lunch yet and might bite back." Everyone liked him, even with his corny sense of humor.

The last time I saw him was just before Christmas. He was his same old jovial, slightly nutty self. His heart rate was controlled but still irregular. As I finished listening to his heart, he said, "I've been thinking about donating my heart to science, Doc. Do you think they would take it?"

"I think you still have a few more years to use it, Mr. Green," I said smiling at him.

"I'm glad to hear it, Doc. I just have to figure out what to use it for." He picked up his hat and twisted it in his left hand, then reached out to shake my hand with his right. "See ya next month, if I can find my way back." He turned and walked down the hall, waving to all the staff. I chuckled to myself and moved on to the next patient.

The next morning, Janice came to me and said, "There is a woman on the phone who says she needs to talk to you about Mr. Green."

"I just saw him yesterday." I picked up the phone. "This is Dr. Morris."

The voice on the other end said, "Are you Willie Green's doctor?"

"Yes ma'am, I am."

"I just wanted to tell you that he passed during the night."

"What?" I exclaimed. "He was fine when he left here."

"I know," she said. "He was fine when he went to bed, but he never woke up."

My mind began to race. What could have happened? I immediately thought about that irregular heartbeat. Maybe it had led to a blood clot, which then caused a massive stroke. Medically it made sense, but I was sick to my stomach, realizing he had died.

I paused for a moment then said, "Thank you for calling. How did you know Mr. Green?" I asked the question because I sensed something was out of the ordinary. I was fairly certain that the woman I was talking to was an African-American, while Mr. Green was Anglo. Who was this woman and why was she calling me about him?

"About six years ago I found him on the street. He looked pretty bad, but I could tell he had a kind heart. I brought him home, cleaned him up, and gave him a room he could stay in. He was really never much trouble except that he was a little trouble when he was drinking, but we got that under control after a while. He would work out of the labor pool and pay me a little money from time to time for food and rent, but he was good company to have around. Occasionally he would fix things for me, but he always liked talking more than fixin'."

"You were kind to look out for him," I said.

"He was no trouble. I thought you would like to know that the funeral will be on Friday at the Ford Funeral Home at one o'clock."

Once again I could sense something was not right. The Ford Funeral Home is a huge operation but was used almost exclusively by African-Americans.

"Who is paying for the funeral?" I asked.

She paused for a second, then answered, "Over the years, I saved a little money up from the rent he gave me, so I thought I would use that to pay the expense. I hope you will come; he always spoke highly of you and the Church Clinic."

I thanked her for calling and we hung up.

When Friday came, as soon as I finished seeing patients in the morning, I rushed over to the funeral home. I felt conspicuous as I walked into the front hall.

There was a young girl sitting at the front desk and I asked her, "Do you know where Mr. Willie Green is?"

"No," she said. I was surprised.

Not seeing anyone else to ask, I began to wander around the halls. I quickly came upon an open casket in a small room. I immediately recognized Mr. Green. He was laid out with his hair combed and his hands folded over his chest. He was wearing a tan suit and looked like a true gentleman.

I thought to myself, "I bet Willie Green hasn't had a suit on in 30 years." At any rate, he looked pretty good. I stood over the casket for a few moments; then I went over to sign the visitation book. When I picked up the pen my heart sank slightly as I realized there was only one other name ahead of mine. I looked at it closely—Easter Holmes. It sounded familiar, but I wasn't sure.

I left the funeral home and drove back to the clinic. My mind was filled with thoughts of Willie Green and his caretaker.

As I began to prepare to resume seeing patients, I told Debbie about my experience. When I finished describing the events at the visitation book, she said, "You do know that Easter Holmes is also one of your patients, and she is the woman who called you about Mr. Green?"

I was stunned. I didn't know what to say. I could not place her, yet felt humbled by the acts of charity this woman had performed for a man she "found on the street."

Since that day I have made sure I know and recognize Easter Holmes whenever she comes to the Church Health Center. She is a simple woman who is always friendly. She is quick to smile and patient if she ever has to wait.

I have spoken to her on several occasions about her relationship with Willie Green. She always returns to the refrain, "He was really not much trouble. He was just a child of God."

I often wonder at the irony that a woman named Easter revealed to me in such a dramatic way the true meaning of what being a servant of God is all about. Her unselfish gifts to Willie Green were more than most of us would be able to give—more than I am able to give. But I am dedicated to the belief that though we may not all be able to sacrifice in the way that Easter has, at least we can find a way to care for her when she is sick or in need of the services we have to offer. We can care for Easter and for anyone like Willie whom she would bring to us. In the final analysis, they are really not much trouble. They are just children of God.

Conclusion

For the last thirteen years I have attempted to live out my own sense of calling as both a physician and a minister through the work of the Church Health Center. Although I grew up in an affluent suburb of Atlanta, today I spend the majority of my waking hours with the working poor of Memphis. I have known all along that I have professional skills which I can offer to those who come for help, but I have wondered and doubted whether I have very much to give in the realm of pastoral care to the people I treat. As it has turned out, these thirteen years have been a journey on which I have been taught the lessons of life by the people I have come to know as a result of being their doctor. Many of them have shown me that the way to true discipleship can be painful and disturbing. Phen Phong comes to mind. In others I have seen a simple trust in God or Jesus which has sustained them in a greater measure than my sophisticated theology ever could. Here I think of Annie.

For many, if not for most, their lives, like mine, bring them in and out of contact with the divine. Often, touching something greater than ourselves happens when we are just doing our jobs. The time I observed Merilyn holding the elderly woman in her arms is a perfect example.

Several years ago I discovered a passage from Paul's letter to the Colossians that I try to read to myself everyday. It helps me prepare for the unexpected and forces me to think intentionally of being a follower of Christ. Paul writes, "You are the people of God; he loved you and chose you for his own. So then, you must clothe yourselves with compassion, kindness, humility, gentleness and patience" (Col. 3:12, TEV).

These five manners of being now define how I try to live and see the world. Each day I see, in a new way, patients' reflections of these manners. Each story I have told in this book either has developed my understanding of compassion and gentleness, or reflects on an experience which changed me in my feeling for this way of life that is set forth for the people of God.

I am never sure whether I will live each day able to generate kindness and mercy in my own heart. But the wonder of the Church Health Center has been that I know that these manners of the life of faith will be all around me as I go about my duties. Patients, staff, and volunteers in varied ways will enfold me somehow through the course of events. This is a truly comforting thought, the knowledge of which helps hold my feet on the path of discipleship.